THE USA 1929–1980

GCSE Modern World History for Edexcel

Steve Waugh
John Wright

HODDER
EDUCATION
PART OF HACHETTE LIVRE UK

The Publishers would like to thank the following for permission to reproduce copyright material:

Photo credits
p.6 *l* © Corbis, *r* © Corbis; **p.9** Culver Pictures; **p.11** *t* © Bettmann/Corbis, *b* Mary Evans Picture Library; **p.15** *t* © Corbis, *b* Peter Newark's American Pictures; **p.18** © Bettmann/Corbis; **p.19** AP/Wide World Photos; **p.22** © Bettmann/Corbis; **p.25** Topfoto/AP; **p.28** © Bettmann/Corbis; **p.29** © Bettmann/Corbis; **p.31** © Bettmann/Corbis; **p.32** Peter Newark's American Pictures; **p.34** photo courtesy FDR Library; **p.35** photo courtesy FDR Library; **p.37** © New York Daily News, L.P. reprinted with permission; **p.38** Brown Brothers; **p.39** Peter Newark's American Pictures; **p.40** Brown Brothers; **p.41** © Bettmann/Corbis; **p.42** *t & b* courtesy Tennessee Valley Authority; **p.43** © Bettmann/Corbis; **p.44** © Bettmann/Corbis; **p.49** © Corbis; **p.52** © Bettmann/Corbis; **p.53** *tl, tr & b* © Bettmann/Corbis; **p.54** Punch Library & Archive; **p.57** © The Washington Post, photo courtesy Library of Congress, Clifford Berryman Collection (LC-USZ62-17312); **p.58** reprinted by permission of J. N. "Ding" Darling Foundation; **p.61** photo courtesy FDR Library; **p.62** Peter Newark's American Pictures; **p.64** AP/Wide World Photos; **p.65** © Bettmann/Corbis; **p.67** The Art Archive/National Archives; **p.68** © Bettmann/Corbis; **p.70** © Bettmann/Corbis; **p.71** © Bettmann/Corbis; **p.72** © Corbis; **p.73** Popperfoto.com; **p.75** *t* © Bettmann/Corbis, *b* © Library of Congress (LC-USZ62-36154); **p.77** Library of Congress; **p.79** © Bettmann/Corbis; **p.85** © Picture History; **p.86** The Moviestore Collection; **p.87** *l* Getty Images, *r* © Corbis; **p.88** Library of Congress (LC-USW3-034282-C); **p.89** *l* Getty Images, *r* © Bettmann/Corbis; **p.90** AP/ Wide World Photos; **p.92** *t* © Leonard Freed/Magnum Photos, *b* © Elliott Erwitt/Magnum Photos; **p.93** © Bettmann/Corbis; **p.94** AP/ Wide World Photos; **p.95** © Bettmann/Corbis; **p.96** AP/Wide World Photos; **p.98** © Bettmann/Corbis; **p.99** AP/ Wide World Photos; **p.100** © Bettmann/Corbis; **p.102** © Bettmann/Corbis; **p.103** © Bettmann/Corbis; **p.104** © Bob Adelman/Magnum Photos; **p.107** Time Life Pictures/Getty Images; **p.108** © Ted Spiegel/Corbis; **p.109** Topfoto; **p.113** LBJ Library photo by Yoichi R. Okamoto; **p.115** Punch Library & Archive; **p.118** *l* © Ted Spiegel/Corbis, *r* LBJ Library photo by Yoichi R. Okamoto; **p.119** © Jerry Schatzberg/Corbis; **p.120** © Bettmann/Corbis; **p.121** © Jerry Schatzberg/Corbis; **p.122** © Bettmann/Corbis; **p.123** *l* Getty Images, *r* © Henry Diltz/Corbis; **p.125** © Bettmann/Corbis; **p.128** AP/Wide World Photos; **p.130** *tl & tr* AP/Wide World Photos, *bl* © Bettmann/Corbis, *br* Getty Images; **p.133** from *Herblock Special Report* (W.W. Norton, 1984) reproduced courtesy of The Herb Block Foundation; **p.134** © Bettmann/Corbis; **p.136** from *Herblock: A Cartoonist's Life* (Times Books, 1998) reproduced courtesy of The Herb Block Foundation; **p.137** Topfoto/AP; **p.140** © Bettmann/Corbis.

Acknowledgements
Edexcel for exam questions from the June, 2004 paper; The National Archives and Records Administration for an extract from a letter by Harry S Truman, 18th August 1948; The New Republic for an extract from *The New Deal in Review 1936–40*, 1940; Newsweek magazine for an extract from 'The Intent of the CCC', 8th April 1933, © 1933 Newsweek, Inc. All rights reserved. Reprinted by permission; Oxford University Press for an extract from 'Psalm 23' by E J Sullivan, from *The Depression and the New Deal: A History in Documents* by Robert S McElvaine, 2000; Special Rider Music for the lyrics from 'Oxford Town', Copyright © 1963 by Warner Bros. Inc. Copyright renewed 1991 by Special Rider Music. All rights reserved. International copyright secured. Reprinted by permission, and 'Blowin' In The Wind', Copyright © 1962 by Warner Bros. Inc. Copyright renewed 1990 by Special Rider Music. All rights reserved. International copyright secured. Reprinted by permission; Stormking Music for lyrics from 'I Don't Want Your Millions Mister' by Jim Garland, © Stormking Music Inc. Rights administered by Harmony Music Limited.

The publishers would also like to thank the following for permission to reproduce graphs and charts in this book:
The British Association for American Studies for 'Appointment of Officials' from *Impatient for Justice*, C Barnes, Longman; Harcourt Education for 'Selected share prices' from *The Modern World History* by M Chandler and J Wright. Reprinted by permission; HarperCollins Ltd for a graph of 'Sales of stocks and shares on New York Stock Exchange' from *USA 1917–75*, by Harriet Ward, © Harriet Ward; Hodder Education for a graph from *USA Between the Wars 1919–41*, by T Fiehn, M Samuelson, R Mills and C White; Oxford University Press for the figures 'Share increases', 'Suicides per 100,000 people', 'Bank collapses' and 'Roosevelt's economic theory', © Oxford University Press 1996, from *The USA 1917–1980* by Nigel Smith (OUP, 1996). Reprinted by permission; Pearson Education for 'US GNP 1927–41' from *Roosevelt and the United States*, by O'Callaghan, and 'Earnings and prices in the USA 1920–1941' from *The Making of America*, by Beacroft and Smale, © Pearson Education Limited.

Every effort has been made to trace all copyright holders, but if any have been inadvertently overlooked the Publishers will be pleased to make the necessary arrangements at the first opportunity.

Although every effort has been made to ensure that website addresses are correct at time of going to press, Hodder Murray cannot be held responsible for the content of any website mentioned in this book. It is sometimes possible to find a relocated web page by typing in the address of the home page for a website in the URL window of your browser.

Orders: please contact Bookpoint Ltd, 130 Milton Park, Abingdon, Oxon OX14 4SB. Telephone: (44) 01235 827720. Fax: (44) 01235 400454. Lines are open 9.00–5.00, Monday to Saturday, with a 24-hour message answering service. Visit our website at www.hoddereducation.co.uk

© Steve Waugh and John Wright, 2005
First published in 2005 by
Hodder Education,
part of Hachette Livre UK,
338 Euston Road
London NW1 3BH

Impression number   10 9 8 7 6 5
Year   2010 2009 2008

Cover photos: Henry Guttmann/Getty Images (left) and Bettmann/CORBIS (right)
Typeset in Garamond by Fakenham Photosetting Limited, Fakenham, Norfolk
Printed in Italy

A catalogue record for this title is available from the British Library

ISBN-13: 978 0 340 88903 9

Contents

Introduction

This book covers a fascinating period in the history of the USA. A period during which:

- The wealthiest country in the world in the 1920s suffered from a serious depression in the years after 1929.
- A senator called Joe McCarthy carried out a witch-hunt against anyone suspected of having communist sympathies.
- One president was assassinated and another one was nearly put on trial by Congress.
- Black Americans, women and students all campaigned in various ways for improved rights.

Read on. In this textbook you will find out more about these events and study other key developments in the USA during the period 1929–1980.

About the course

During this course you must study two outline studies, two depth studies and two coursework units. There are two written exam papers:

- In Paper 1 you have two hours to answer questions on two outline studies.
- In Paper 2 you have one hour and 45 minutes to answer questions on two depth studies.

Outline studies (Paper 1)

Outline studies cover a relatively long period of change and development. It could be:

- Developments in the Soviet Union, from the purges and mass killings of the Stalinist regime in the 1920s and 1930s to the amazing events of the late 1980s when the Soviet Union collapsed.
- Key events in the Cold War, from the end of the Second World War to 1991. How close did the world come to nuclear war?

In this book, Chapters 6–11 cover the key information and skills needed for the outline study *The Divided Union? The USA, 1941–80.* You will be able to decide for yourself whether it really was the 'divided union' and make judgements on the following issues:

- Why, in a so-called democracy, were people hounded out of their jobs because of their political beliefs in the 1950s?
- Why were black Americans still treated as second-class citizens in the 1950s and 1960s?
- Why did some women burn their bras in public in the 1960s?
- Why are many Americans fascinated by the life and death of John F Kennedy?
- What involvement did a US president have with a break-in?

Paper 1 is a test of:

- Knowledge and understanding of the key developments in each outline study.
- Ability to write brief and extended essay type questions.

You will have to write brief and more extended essays which ask you to demonstrate the following historical skills:

- Causation – why something happened
- Consequence – the effects or results of an event
- Change – how much change took place and why the change happened
- Describe – a detailed description usually of the key events in a given period.

Chapters 6–11 will give you detailed guidance on how best to approach and answer the types of questions that you will be asked in Paper 1.

Depth studies (Paper 2)

In these you are given the opportunity to study a much shorter period but in greater depth. This could be:

- Nazi Germany, 1930–39, including Hitler's rise to power and the creation of a Nazi state in the years before the outbreak of the Second World War. What was the Night of the Long Knives?
- Russia in the period 1910–24. How was a small minority party, the Bolsheviks, able to seize power in 1917?
- The War in Vietnam, 1963–75. How and why did the USA become involved? Why did it have such a devastating effect on the USA and Vietnam itself?

Chapters 1–5 in this book cover the key information and skills needed for *Depression and the New Deal: the USA, 1929–41* which is a popular depth study. It is often studied alongside the USA outline study.

Paper 2 is a test of:

- Knowledge and understanding of a shorter period in history.
- Ability to answer four different types of source questions.

In order to answer Paper 2 questions successfully, you will need to have generic and question-specific source skills:

- 'Generic source skills' refers to your ability to examine the nature, origins and purpose of sources.
- 'Question-specific source skills' refers to the four different types of source questions. These are:
  - inference
  - cross-referencing
  - utility
  - the ability to discuss an interpretation.

Chapters 1–5 will give you detailed guidance on how best to approach and answer these types of questions, and help you to build up gradually the source skills you need.

About the book

The book is divided into two main sections:

- The first section covers the depth study: *Depression and the New Deal: the USA, 1929–41.* It includes an introduction explaining the key areas of knowledge and understanding and an explanation of the general source skills you will need. It is then divided into five chapters which cover the key events and which contain activities to develop, step-by-step, the source skills you will need.
- The second section covers the outline study: *A Divided Union? The USA, 1941–80.* It includes an introduction explaining the key themes and areas of knowledge and understanding you will need. It is then divided into six chapters which give you in-depth knowledge about each of these themes and which contain activities to help develop, step-by-step, the exam skills you will need.

Each chapter in this book:

- Contains activities – some help develop the historical skills you will need, others are exam-style questions which give you the opportunity to practise exam skills.
- Gives step-by-step guidance, model answers and advice on how to answer particular question types.
- Defines key terms and highlights glossary terms in bold the first time they appear in either the outline study or depth study sections.

Depression and the New Deal: the USA, 1929–41

An unemployed man on a park bench in Washington DC, 1930.

Workers in the Civilian Conservation Corps with President Roosevelt in 1933.

Task

What is the contrast between these two photographs?

This depth study tries to explain the contrast shown in the two photographs by examining the impact of the Wall Street Crash and the Depression upon the economy and the people of the USA, and the attempts made by President Roosevelt to tackle this Depression. Each chapter explains a key issue and poses certain questions as shown below.

Chapter 1 The causes and consequences of the Wall Street Crash (pages 9–20)

- What happened to the US economy during the 1920s?
- What was consumerism and the share boom? Who benefited from these?
- What were the long-term and more immediate causes of the Wall Street Crash?
- What effects did the Crash have on the USA?

Chapter 2 The impact of the Depression, 1929–33 (pages 21–32)

- How were the economy and American people affected by the Depression?
- Why did President Hoover not do more to ease the worst effects of the Depression?
- Who were the Bonus Marchers?
- Why did Roosevelt win the presidential election campaign of 1932?

Chapter 3 Attempts at recovery: the New Deal (pages 33–48)

- What was meant by the New Deal?
- What policies did Roosevelt introduce to deal with agriculture, industry, unemployment and welfare?
- What were the TVA and the dust bowl?

Chapter 4 Opposition to the New Deal (pages 49–58)

- Why was there opposition to the New Deal from Republicans and businessmen?
- Why did certain key individuals oppose the New Deal?
- Why did Roosevelt face opposition from the Supreme Court? How did he deal with this opposition?

Chapter 5 The successes and failures of the New Deal (pages 59–63)

- What were the achievements and limitations of the New Deal?
- What impact did it have on: the role of government and the president, the economy, unemployment, industrial workers, social welfare, black Americans and women?

Depth study questions

In the examination you will be given six sources and have to answer four source questions. Here are the questions on this depth study from the June 2004 exam.

EXAM

PAPER 2 The USA Depth Study

(a) Study Source A.
What can you learn from Source A about the effects of the New Deal on the people of the USA?

(4 marks)

(b) Study Sources A, B and C.
Does Source C support the evidence of Sources A and B about the effects of the New Deal on the people of the USA? Explain your answer.

(6 marks)

(c) Study Sources D and E.
How useful are these two sources as evidence about the changes brought about by the New Deal?

(8 marks)

(d) Study all the Sources.
'By 1941 the New Deal had been successful in solving all the problems caused by the Depression'.
Use the sources and your own knowledge to explain whether you agree with this view.

(12 marks)

(Total 30 marks)

This is called an **inference** question. This means getting a message or messages from the source.

This is a **utility** question – you must decide how useful a source is.

This is a **cross-referencing** question – asking you to compare the views of the three sources.

This is called a **synthesis** question – it asks you to use the sources and your own knowledge to discuss an interpretation.

You will be given step-by-step guidance in how to answer all these types of questions in Chapters 1–5.

Generic source skills

Look at the four questions on the previous page. You will have to answer each of these four types of question for each of your depth studies in Paper 2. In order to answer these source questions you need to have some basic, general source skills. You need to be confident in examining the NOP of sources. This stands for the:

Nature
Origin
Purpose

Examining the NOP of sources will encourage you to ask questions, set out below.

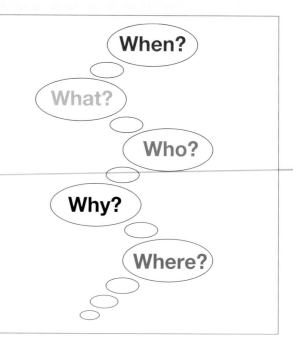

When?

What?

Who?

Why?

Where?

Nature

- What type of source is it?

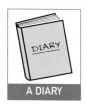 A DIARY

 LETTER

 PHOTOGRAPH

 NEWSPAPER REPORT

 SPEECH

 CARTOON, ETC

- How will this influence the utility (usefulness) of the source?
- For example, cartoons exaggerate, but does that mean they are not useful?

Origins

- Who produced the source? What do I know about this person or organisation?
- When was the source produced?
- Is this person or organisation likely to give a one-sided view of the event? If so, which side is not represented?

- Is it the evidence of an eyewitness? What are the advantages and disadvantages of eyewitness evidence?
- Was it written at a later date? Did the person have the benefit of hindsight?
- What are the advantages and limitations of sources that were written later?
- Under what circumstances or in what situation was the source produced? For example, some sources are written under strict government control and censorship. The person who wrote the source might not have the freedom to write what they genuinely believe.

Purpose

- Why was the source produced, written, drawn, etc?
- Is the person trying to make you support one view or one side? For example, most speeches are made by people who are trying to convince others of their views.
- Is the source an example of propaganda? If so, what view is it trying to get across?
- Be careful, propaganda sources are useful because they provide evidence of the methods used.

Chapters 1–5 will help develop these generic source skills using a variety of sources and tasks.

The causes and consequences of the Wall Street Crash

1

Source A A seaside resort, USA, 4 July 1926

Tasks

Study Source A.

1. *What can you learn from the photograph about the USA in the 1920s? Make a judgement about the photograph – do not simply describe what you see.*

2. *What do you think are the weaknesses of the source? Does the date help you answer this?*

The First World War (1914–18) had a considerable impact on the USA – its economy prospered as the demand for food, raw materials and manufactured goods increased. At the end of the war, the USA emerged as the strongest economic power in the world. It had loaned $10.3 billion during the war to its allies – and nine-tenths of this had been used to buy American goods. American farmers were exporting three times as much food to Europe in 1918 as in 1914. The 1920s saw much of the USA experience a time of prosperity when the 'American dream' seemed to be in the grasp of many of its citizens.

This chapter will answer the following questions:

• Why did the USA prosper in the 1920s?
• Why was there a share boom in the 1920s?
• Who was excluded from the boom?

• Why was there a 'Crash'? (This is the start of the main content for the depth study.)
• What were the effects of the 'Crash'?

Source skills

In this chapter, you will look at inference questions from Paper 2 but there will also be questions which help develop your understanding of the topic. Do remember that in Paper 2, you will answer questions which focus not only on your source skills but will also examine your knowledge and understanding of a topic.

Why did the USA prosper during the 1920s'

Three Republican Presidents

In the 1920s the presidents of the USA were all **Republicans**, which meant that they held similar political and economic views. They were:

• Warren Harding: 1921–23
• Calvin Coolidge: 1923–29
• Herbert Hoover: 1929–33

Harding said he would return the USA '**back to normalcy**' but he was only president for two years, dying suddenly in 1923. Directly after his death, it was revealed that he had been involved in financial scandals with his close associates. Coolidge succeeded Harding and he carried on the policy of limiting the role of government in the economy and reducing the tax burden on the rich. Hoover, the millionaire president, was a self-made man and he was the Republicans' best example of what could be achieved in the USA by hard work and little government interference.

'The business of America is business'

President Coolidge said this in 1924 and, indeed, in the 1920s most Americans believed that governments should be involved as little as possible in the day-to-day running of the economy. If businessmen were left alone to make their own decisions, it was thought that high profits, more jobs and good wages would be the result. This was the policy of *laissez-faire* – the only role for the government was to help business when it was asked to.

Under Harding and Coolidge, the Republican economic policy of *laissez-faire* contributed to the prosperity of the USA. Low taxes and few regulations meant that businessmen were able to chase profits without fear of interference. Nevertheless, the government of this period did act twice to intervene in the economy:

• The Fordney–McCumber Tariff (1922) raised **import duties** on goods coming into the USA to

---

Back to normalcy

Harding's slogan promised a return to the more carefree days of 1917– before the US entered the First World War.

Consumer goods

Manufactured items purchased by people.

Credit

The facility of borrowing money over a given period.

Import duties

Taxes placed on goods brought from foreign countries.

Income tax

Payment from wages/salaries to the government treasury.

Laissez-faire

A policy of no direct government interference in the economy.

Mass production

The manufacture of the same item on an assembly line, where the workers carry out the same task as the item passes before them.

Republican

Supporter of the Republican Party. Its main ideas were to keep taxes low, limit the powers of the Federal government (see page 23), follow policies which favoured business and encourage people to be self-sufficient.

---

the highest level ever, thus protecting American industry and encouraging Americans to buy home-produced goods.
• A reduction of **income tax** rates left some people with more cash to spend on **consumer goods**. This, in turn, provided the cash to buy the home-produced goods.

Consumerism

As profits increased, so did wages (though by nothing like so much). Between 1923 and 1929, the average wage rose by eight per cent. Though this was not spectacular, it was enough to enable some workers to buy – often on **credit** (also called hire purchase) – the new consumer luxuries in Source A. The development of advertising and radio commercials in the 1920s, such as the advert in Source B, encouraged people to buy these new goods.

At the start of the 1920s, the USA experienced another industrial revolution. One reason for this was widespread use of electrical power. In 1912, only sixteen per cent of the American people lived in electrically-lit homes. By 1927, the number had risen to 63 per cent. The growth of electric power encouraged a much more widespread use of electrical goods such as irons, ovens, washing machines, vacuum cleaners, refrigerators, radios and telephones. During this period, consumption of other energy sources also grew, for example the amount of oil used doubled and gas quadrupled.

The impact of the automobile

A Ford production line. Can you suggest why Ford was able to produce cheap automobiles (cars)?

The product which had the greatest impact on American life was the automobile. Henry Ford developed the system of **mass production** which enabled him to make huge quantities of vehicles. This revolutionised American industry – indeed it revolutionised American society:

* The car industry used so much steel, wood, petrol, rubber and leather that it provided jobs for more than five million people.
* It transformed American buying habits, making hire purchase a way of life for most Americans because it enabled an average family to buy a car.
* It promoted road building and travel, which in turn led to hotels and restaurants being built in places that had been considered out of the way.

The production of automobiles rose dramatically from 1.9 million in 1920, to 4.5 million in 1929. The three main manufacturers were the giant firms of Ford, Chrysler and General Motors.

Source A: Growth in sales of consumer goods

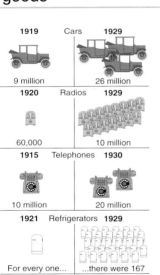

1919	Cars	1929
9 million		26 million
1920	Radios	**1929**
60,000		10 million
1915	Telephones	**1930**
10 million		20 million
1921	Refrigerators	**1929**
For every one...		...there were 167

Source B: Advert for a vacuum cleaner in the 1920s

Tasks

1. *What can you learn about the economy of the USA in the 1920s from Source A?*

2. *What can you learn from Source B about advertisements in the USA in the 1920s?*

Task

3. *Make a list of the reasons why the USA was prosperous in the 1920s.*

* *Look at the list and now list the reasons again, in order of importance.*

* *Explain why each reason was important in making the USA prosperous in the 1920s.*

Why was there a share boom in the 1920s?

The rise of the stock market

In the 1920s, the **stock market** seemed to be the link to the prosperity of the USA. The values of **stocks and shares** rose steadily throughout the decade until they rose dramatically in 1928 and 1929. Moreover, the amount of buying and selling of shares grew substantially until it was a common occurrence for ordinary working people to become involved – the accepted image of the 1920s is that 'even the shoeshine boy' was dealing in shares.

Most companies' shares seemed to rise, and so people were prepared to risk their money on buying shares – after all, their value would rise. The USA began to speculate. Even if people did not have enough money to pay the full amount, they would make a deposit, borrow to pay the rest and then sell the shares in a couple of weeks when their value had risen and a profit had been made. The speculator would then pay off his debt and still have made money on the deal. (This was called 'buying on the margin'.)

The number of shares traded in 1926 was about 451 million, increasing to 577 million the following year. By 1928, with share prices rising fast, there was a **bull market** on the **Wall Street Stock Exchange** and, in 1929, there were more than 1.1 billion shares sold. Up to 25 million Americans became involved in the frenzy of share dealing in the last years of the decade. The graph below illustrates how quickly sales in shares grew.

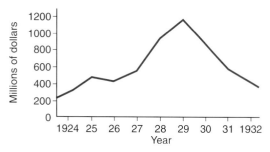

Graph showing sales of stocks and shares on the Wall Street Stock Exchange, 1923–32.

Key Terms

Bull market
A time when share prices are rising.

Democratic Party
One of the two main political parties. The party is likely to agree with federal government intervention.

Stock market
The place where stocks and shares were bought and sold on a daily basis.

Stocks and shares
Certificates of ownership in a company.

Wall Street Stock Exchange
New York's stock market was based here.

Company	31 August 1928	3 September 1929	29 October 1929
American and Foreign Power	$38.00	$167.75	$73.00
AT and T	$182.00	$304.00	$230.00
Hershey Chocolate	$53.25	$128.00	$108.00
IBM	$130.86	$241.75	–
People's Gas, Chicago	$182.86	$182.86	–
Detroit Edison	$205.00	$350.00	–

Selected share prices, 1927–29. Why would these figures encourage people to buy shares *before* September 1929?

Speculation

Advice like that offered in Source A (on the following page) encouraged many to invest in the stock market. Banks at the time were usually paying an annual interest rate of seven per cent on savings accounts. The difference between the return on savings and speculation made the stock market seem an attractive gamble. If a person was prepared to speculate on the market then lots of money could be made. Buying shares 'on the margin' fuelled speculation further.

Frequently, investors borrowed money to buy shares, but as long as share prices continued to rise then there was nothing to worry about. People were so confident about the market that, by the summer of 1929, investors had borrowed $8.5 billion to buy on the margin – a figure that had risen from $3.2 billion in 1926.

Source A: John J Raskob, leading Democratic Party politician, speaking about the benefit of buying shares in 1928

If a man saves $15 a week, and invests in good shares . . . at the end of twenty years [he] will have at least $80,000 and an income from investments of around $400 a month.

Source B: From *After the Crash* by J Rublowsky, 1970, describing the share buying frenzy

Almost any share was gobbled up in the hope of striking it rich but many of these were worthless. The Seabord Airline was actually a railroad and had nothing to do with aviation, yet it attracted thousands of investors because aviation shares were the glamour issue of the day.

Source C: From *The Lawless Decade* by P Sann, 1958, on speculation

Speculation wasn't gambling, it was an investment in the glorious American future, an expression of faith in the endless wondrous prosperity that blessed the land.

Tasks

1. What can you learn from sources A–C about people who were involved in share dealing in the USA in the 1920s?

2. On the right is a concept map showing some reasons for the increase in selling/buying shares.

• Copy the concept map and suggest other reasons for the increases by completing the blank boxes.

• Add new boxes or ones linked to those already there with more reasons.

Prohibition

• In 1919, the 18th Amendment to the US constitution forbade the 'manufacture, sale or transport of intoxicating liquors' throughout the country. Many religious groups had been keen to introduce prohibition, as had the Anti-Saloon League and also Women's organisations.

• Prohibition was not successful because it was easy to set up secret drinking places – 'speakeasies'. Drink was sold on the black market for very high prices and the whole business saw the emergence of gangsters. Men such as Al Capone made fortunes out of smuggling and selling 'illegal alcohol'.

• Prohibition added to the misery of farmers (see the next page) because their crops were no longer needed – barley and hops. Even those involved in growing grapes suffered. Hoover did little to stop the gangsters and it was left to Roosevelt to end prohibition in 1933.

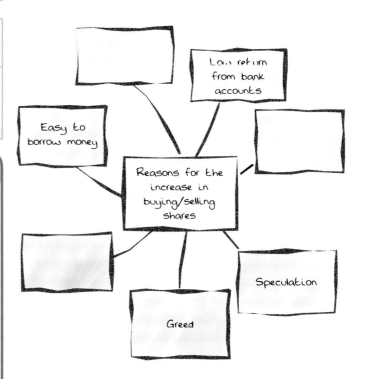

Who was excluded from the boom?

Poverty in the midst of plenty

Source A: A Republican Party election leaflet 1928

A Chicken *for* Every Pot

During eight years of rule we have built more homes, erected more skyscrapers, passed more laws to regulate and purify immigration, done more to increase production, expand export markets, and reduce industrial and human junk piles, than in any previous quarter century. Prosperity is written on fuller wage packets, written in factory chimney smoke, written on walls of new constructions, written in bank books, written in business profit sheets, and written in the record value of shares.

Wages, dividends
progress and prosperity say,
"Vote *for* Hoover"

Despite all the signs of prosperity and the mood of optimism in the 1920s, all was not as it seemed. There were ominous cracks beneath the surface. Many people did not share in the country's expanding wealth. There were people in **urban ghettos** and in rural areas who were easily overlooked as they struggled to make ends meet.

Very real poverty continued to exist, among the unskilled immigrants in the big cities, among farmers and among the African-Americans in both the North and the deep South. They were second-class citizens – low paid, undernourished and badly housed. In 1929, the average wage in the North-East was $881 a year, but in the South-East it was $365 a year. It has been estimated that about 70 million out of 110 million Americans were living below the **poverty line** in the 1920s. The elderly, disabled and many immigrants were not a part of the prosperity – there were no pensions or state benefits to act as a safety net.

Farmers

- After the war, farmers took out mortgages worth $2 billion in an attempt to stave off disaster.
- Many soon became so indebted that their farms passed on to **creditors** and the farmers became tenants on land they had once owned.
- The income of the farm labourer even in the

Key Terms

Congress

The USA equivalent of parliament is Congress. Congress is split into two parts, the **Senate** and the **House of Representatives**. Anyone elected to either house is called a congressman.

Creditor

One to whom a financial debt is owed.

Lynching

Mob action in which a person is executed without a trial.

Migrate

To move from one part of the country to another.

Poverty line

The income level at which a family is unable to meet its basic needs.

Price-fixing

Agreement to charge the same or a similar price for goods.

Urban ghettos

Town/city area consisting of a minority who live there because of social and economic pressures.

Veto

The right of the president to block a piece of legislation.

most affluent years of the 1920s was generally only about half that of coal miners and not much more than one-quarter of clerical workers.

Farmers had come to depend on selling produce abroad. Yet the government had not helped by raising import duties on foreign goods which caused other countries to do the same. This meant that American farmers saw the price of their produce increase and become uncompetitive abroad. On several occasions, a bill was introduced to help grain farmers (later bills included tobacco

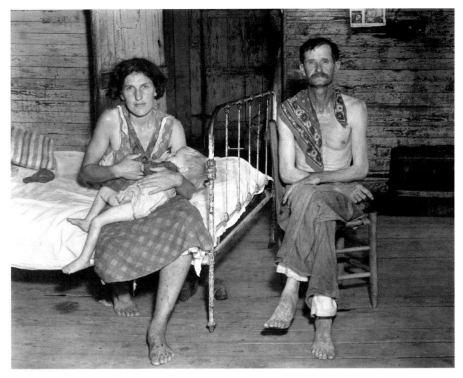

Rural poverty in Alabama. What evidence of poverty is there in the photograph?

and cotton producers), and in 1927 and 1928 the McNary–Haugen Bill passed through **Congress**, only to be **vetoed** by President Coolidge. Coolidge felt the Bill involved **price-fixing** and benefited only certain groups; moreover he wanted to limit the role of the government.

McNary–Haugen Bill

- A Federal Farm Board was to be created to purchase surplus farm produce at pre-First World War prices; the surpluses were to be stored until domestic conditions improved or until a decision was made to sell them on world markets.

- If the Farm Board made a loss in selling the surpluses, then compensation would be given to the farmers.

Black Americans

At the end of the First World War, many black Americans in the North lost their jobs to returning soldiers. Few enjoyed the industrial boom of the 1920s and there was little improvement in their quality of life. Approximately 825,000 black Americans **migrated** from the rural South to towns and cities in the North, but they still experienced

discrimination in employment, housing and education.

As a result, they turned to such organisations as the National Association for the Advancement of Coloured People (NAACP), the National Urban League (NUL) and the Universal **Negro** Improvement League (UNIA). Though these challenged discrimination and sought to secure increased employment opportunities, little progress was made. The average income for most black Americans during this decade was about $200 a year.

The most appalling treatment of black Americans at this time was **lynching**. The absence of justice for black Americans can be seen in the number of lynchings in this decade – 262 were reported.

A black shanty town in the 1920s. What evidence of poverty is there in the photograph? Compare this photograph with the one above.

Tasks

1. *Explain why farmers were unable to enjoy a period of prosperity in the 1920s.*

2. *In what ways were some Americans excluded from the prosperity of the 1920s?*

Why was there a 'Crash'?

Source A: **A US economist of the 1920s explaining the fears that some Americans had at that time**

Sooner or later, a crash is coming, and it may be terrific, factories will be shut down, men will be thrown out of work and there will be a serious business depression.

Why do you think the economist felt that there would be problems in the future?

Depression

A period of extended and severe decline in a nation's economy, marked by low production and high unemployment.

Tariff

A tax on foreign goods coming into a country. (An import duty.)

The Wall Street Crash

In the autumn of 1929, the stock market crashed, wiping out the fortunes of many Americans. The Crash ushered in the Great **Depression** of the 1930s – the worst economic decline in the history of the USA. It was a time when millions of Americans could not find work, thousands were turned out of their homes, and many roamed the land in railway wagons. Banks failed and people lost their life's savings.

The Great Depression changed the American way of thinking. The government took a more active role in the peace-time economy than ever before. For the first time, it assumed responsibility for relief.

There were several reasons why the Crash happened in 1929, including:

- Overproduction
- Unequal distribution of wealth
- US **tariff** policy
- Over-speculation on the stock market
- Panic selling in 1929.

Overproduction

The problems created by overproduction are shown in the diagram below.

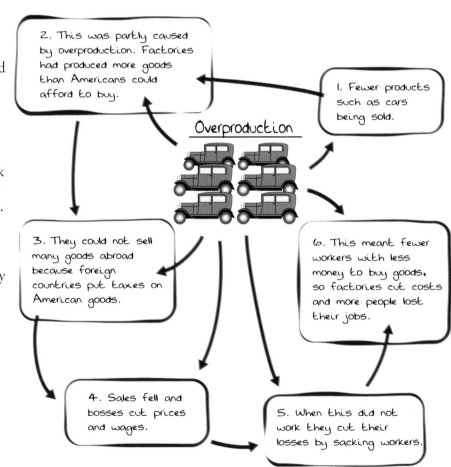

Overproduction

2. This was partly caused by overproduction. Factories had produced more goods than Americans could afford to buy.

1. Fewer products such as cars being sold.

3. They could not sell many goods abroad because foreign countries put taxes on American goods.

6. This meant fewer workers with less money to buy goods, so factories cut costs and more people lost their jobs.

4. Sales fell and bosses cut prices and wages.

5. When this did not work they cut their losses by sacking workers.

Unequal distribution of wealth

The new-found wealth of the 1920s was not shared by everyone. Almost 50 per cent of American families had an income of less than $2,000 a year, the minimum needed to survive. They could not afford to buy the new consumer goods. Some manufacturers did not see that there was a limit to what could be bought, and so they continued to produce goods. The result was overproduction (see previous page).

US tariff policy

The USA could not sell its surplus products to other countries, especially in Europe, for two reasons:

• Some European countries owed the USA huge amounts of money and were struggling with repayments.
• The US government had put high tariffs on foreign goods in the 1920s. Many foreign governments responded by doing the same to American goods and consequently US businessmen found it very difficult to sell their goods abroad. Therefore, an ideal outlet for their overproduction was blocked.

Over-speculation on the stock market

During the 1920s, more and more Americans bought shares on the stock exchange and prices kept rising. In 1928, however, shares did not rise as much as in previous years. This was because many companies were not selling as many goods, so their profits fell. Fewer people were willing to buy their shares and there was a drop in confidence in the market. This was a warning but when share prices began rising again, greed took over and speculation recurred.

Panic selling in 1929

When, in the autumn of 1929, some experts started to sell their shares heavily before their value fell even further, small investors panicked. They saw the fall in prices and rushed to sell their own shares – as can be seen in the bar chart. This led to a complete collapse of prices and thousands of investors lost millions of dollars.

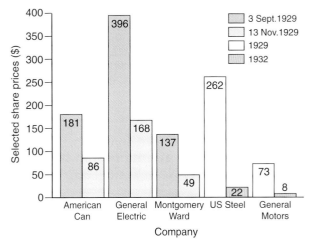

Decline in share values between 1929 and 1932.

Task

Draw your own concept/mind map showing all the major reasons for the Wall Street Crash mentioned on these two pages. Add arrows showing the links between the reasons. Using different colours, briefly explain the links in another label, and clearly connect the label to the arrow. An example has been given below.

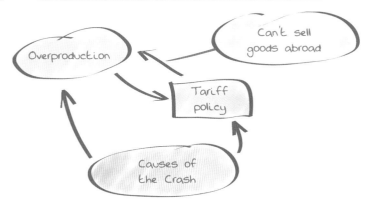

What were the effects of the 'Crash'?

Source A: From *The People, Yes* by C Sandburg, 1936, describing the collapse in share sales

Shares in a cigar company at the time of the crash were selling for $115. The market collapsed and the share dropped to $2 and the company president jumped from his Wall Street office window.

Source B: Depositors trying to withdraw savings at a bank that had closed its doors, New York, 1931

Source C: Suicides in the USA

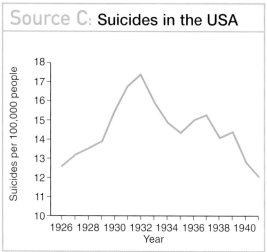

Task

1. What can you learn from sources A, B and C about the effects of the Crash?

Unemployment

The impact of the Crash was quite spectacular. By the end of 1929, there were about 2.5 million unemployed in the USA, although this was only five per cent of the workforce and some felt that the country would see out the crisis. However, confidence had died, and among those who had money there was an unwillingness to spend. Unemployment began to gather pace as fewer and fewer consumer goods were purchased – the amount of goods sold in retail stores halved in the years 1929–33.

Source D: Unemployment 1928–33

Why would President Hoover have been optimistic about the figures for 1933?

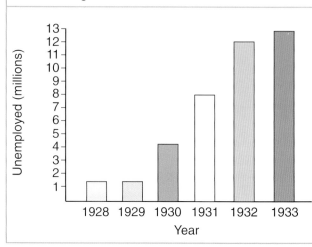

Source E: From *Toledo: A City the Auto Ran Over*, 1 March 1930, compiled by B Amidon. The writer is looking at the impact of the Depression on a US city

When I was taken through some of the eighty-seven buildings that make up the plant I was reminded of the old desert towns left in the wake of the gold rush. There was the same sense of suspended life, as I moved among silent, untended machines or walked through departments where hundreds of half-finished automobile bodies gathered dust.

Source G: From evidence given to Congress in 1931, by the leader of the American Communist Party, about the effects of unemployment on workers in the USA

Thousands of working class families have been thrown out of their homes because they can no longer pay the rent. In the streets of every large city, workers are dropping and dying from starvation and exposure. Every newspaper reports suicides of these workers who are driven to such desperation.

Suddenly the USA became a land of unemployment, tramps, bread queues, and soup kitchens. Many people were evicted from their homes and lived on the streets – children included. It was the time of the **hobo** – thousands of men travelled the country hitching rides on railcars and freight wagons.

Source F: Unemployed queuing for cheap food in New York, 1931

The Depression

People were not buying goods and even the rich began to economise – this meant that employees were laid off. Servants were sacked and those who were able to find jobs worked for lower wages than they had before. The economy was spiralling downwards.

The Depression was not caused by the Crash. The issues with the economy in the 1920s are vital in understanding what was wrong with the US at that time – look once more at pages 10–13. However, the Crash did speed up the approach of the Depression, and its effects were catastrophic for the country and the people during the next decade.

- Many stockbrokers were unable to repay their debts to the banks – many banks went bust.
- Thousands of people who had saved in banks were bankrupted.
- Workforces were laid off.
- There was a collapse of credit and loans were taken in.
- Those banks which survived were unwilling to make further loans – the time of speculation and risk-taking was over.

Farmers were hit terribly, and when they demonstrated in towns they carried placards attacking the president. One slogan became extremely popular: 'In Hoover we trusted, now we are busted.'

Task

2. *Look at the information and sources on pages 18–19. Construct a pyramid/triangle to show a chronology of effects – or a fanning/rippling out of effects – so that the reader can see the chain unfold. The top of the pyramid has been done for you below.*

Crash
Panic

Shares sold · Cash-flow problems

Examination practice

The Crash – it didn't happen in one day. There were a great many warnings. The country was crazy. Everybody was in the stock market, whether he could afford it or not. Shoeshine boys and waiters and capitalists.

Source B: From *America Past and Present,* by Divine, Breen, Frederickson and Williams, 1995, describing the problems of the US economy

The economic system failed to share out wealth fairly. Too much money went into profits and not enough went into the hands of the workers, who were also the consumers. Factory production increased 43 per cent during the 1920s, but the wages of the industrial workers only rose 11 per cent.

Question 1 – inference

What can you learn from Source A about the Wall Street Crash?

How to answer

This is an inference question. You are being asked to give the message of the source, to read between the lines of what is written. For example, in Source A there are several 'messages':

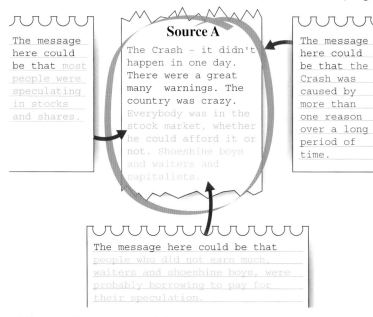

The overall message could be one of over-speculation in the stock market.

Question 2 – inference

What can you learn from Source B about the US economy in the 1920s?

Now have a go yourself

For this kind of question, begin your answer by saying:

'Source B seems to say that . . .' *or*
'Source B implies that . . .' *or*
'Source B suggests that . . .'

In this way you will make a judgement and avoid repeating the content of the source(s). When there is more than one source, remember to quote the source to which you refer.

This should help you to get a message or messages from the source. Look for key words in the source that might lead to inferences. You can also tackle this by copying the source and highlighting different messages in different colours to help you identify the messages contained within.

(2) The impact of the Depression, 1929–33

Source A

From *The Great Republic* by Bailyn, Dallek et al., 1992.

This passage is describing the impact of the Crash

Although the Wall Street Crash did not cause the Depression, the great bull market did trigger it. Consumption dropped. Businesses cut back. Marginal enterprises in farming, banking and business went bankrupt. During the first three years after the Crash, the economy, like a tin can in a vice was relentlessly squeezed to half its size.

Task

What can you learn from Source A about the US economy after the Crash? (Remember what Chapter 1 says about answering inference questions (page 20).)

The impact of the Wall Street Crash and the ensuing economic depression in America was quite spectacular. The land of opportunity rapidly became a land of unemployment, a land of tramps, bread queues, soup kitchens and pessimism. For the average citizen, what happened was totally unfathomable. Within a short time many Americans found themselves homeless, living at the edge of cities in shacks made of tin and old crates. These places became known as 'Hoovervilles'.

In 1932, after twelve years of Republican government, the voters elected a Democratic president, Franklin D Roosevelt, in the hope that America could be pulled out of the mire.

This chapter will answer the following questions:

- How did President Hoover tackle the problems of the economy?
- How did the Depression affect the people of the USA?
- Who were the Bonus Marchers and why were they important?
- Why was Roosevelt elected president in 1932?

Source skills
You will tackle inference and cross-referencing questions from Paper 2.

How did Hoover tackle the economic problems?

Source A: A collection of statements made by Hoover when president

A voluntary deed is infinitely more precious to our national ideal and spirit than a thousand deeds poured from the Treasury.

Each industry should assist its own employees.

Economic wounds must be healed by the producers and consumers themselves.

Each community and each state should assume full responsibility for organisation of employment and relief of distress.

What can you learn from Source A about Hoover's ideas on dealing with the economy?

Hoover had been Secretary for Commerce from 1921–28 and he had tried to follow polices which would end the cycle of boom and bust in business. In the presidential campaign of 1928, he had said: 'The USA is nearer to the final triumph over poverty than ever before in the history of any land'.

Hoover making a speech in 1929. What evidence is there in the photograph to show Hoover's patriotism?

Key Terms

Balance the budget
Ensuring that the government did not spend more than it raised in taxes.

Quaker
Christian religious group devoted to the principles of peace, plainness of speech and dress.

Relief agency
Body set up to help those suffering as a result of the Depression.

Rugged individualism
The American ideal that individuals are responsible for their own lives without help from anyone else; they stand or fall by their own efforts.

Hoover was always optimistic and his **Quaker** upbringing did mean he was a caring person. For example, he gave his presidential salary to victims of the Depression. However, he has been greatly criticised for allowing the economic situation to worsen after 1930 with the onset of the Depression. Nevertheless, Hoover acted quite quickly as the crisis developed and put forward a range of Republican policies to combat the Depression. His reaction was to:

- Continue to **balance the budget**.
- Keep faith with the Republican ideas of *laissez-faire* and '**rugged individualism**'.
- Meet business leaders and ask them not to cut wages or production levels.
- Pass the Hawley–Smoot Tariff Act in 1930. This was to protect US farmers by increasing import duties on foreign goods. In retaliation, other countries refused to reduce trade with the USA.
- Encourage people to give to charities to help the unemployed.
- Suggest that state governments should fund projects to provide new jobs.

- Ensure assistance was given to farmers by the Agricultural Marketing Act of 1930. The act enabled the government to lend some money to farmers through special marketing groups. These tried to stabilise prices and sought to ensure that produce was sold at a profit.
- Set up several agencies for unemployment relief, for example the president's Organisation for Unemployment Relief which aimed to promote and co-ordinate local relief efforts. As a result more than 3,000 offices were opened.
- Won approval from Congress for $1.8 billion for new construction and repairs to roads, dams, etc. across the USA.
- Cut taxes by $130 million.

However, with unemployment continuing to rise in 1931 and 1932, Hoover had to accept that his policies were not working.

He obtained approval from Congress to establish a **relief agency** and the Reconstruction Finance Corporation (RFC) was set up in February 1932, alongside other measures to relieve the crisis (see table below).

Measure	Description
Reconstruction Finance Corporation (February 1932)	Largest federal aid given – $2 billion in loans for ailing banks, insurance companies and railroads. To last only two years and would 'strengthen confidence' and stimulate industry and create jobs.
The Emergency Relief Act (July 1932)	This gave $300 million to state governments to help the unemployed.
Home Loan Bank Act (July 1932)	This was to stimulate house building and home ownership. Twelve regional banks were set up with a fund of $125 million.

By 1932, the federal government was spending $500 million per year more than it had done in 1928. Despite the interference from Hoover and Congress, the economic situation did not improve and, by 1932, there was increasing opposition to Hoover from many quarters in the USA.

Federal v state governments

The USA is a federation or grouping of states with governments which rule themselves and are responsible for local issues such as education. At the centre is an overall **federal government**, represented by the president and Congress, responsible for national issues of defence, taxation, foreign policy. Before Roosevelt, the role of the federal government was seen as very limited.

Source B: From a speech by Andrew Mellon, Hoover's Secretary of the Treasury, January 1930, describing the government's optimism after the Crash

I see nothing in the present situation that is either menacing or warrants pessimism. During the winter months there may be some slackness or unemployment, but hardly more than at this season each year. I have every confidence that there will be a revival of activity in the spring and that during the coming year the country will make steady progress.

Source C: From a popular song of the time, called 'I don't want your millions, Mister'

I don't want your Rolls Royce, Mister,
I don't want your pleasure yacht
All I want is food for my babies
Give me my old job back.
We worked to build this country, Mister
While you enjoyed a life of ease
You've stolen all that we built Mister,
Now our children starve and freeze.

Tasks

1. *Explain why Hoover changed his views in 1932.*

2. *In what ways is Source B limited in helping us to understand the Republicans' reaction to the Crash?*

3. *What can you learn from Source C about the impact of the Depression on some people in the USA?*

How did the Depression affect people?

Source A: A re-wording of Psalm 23, written in 1932 by E J Sullivan who had lived in a Hooverville. He called his verse the 1932nd Psalm

Hoover is our shepherd
We are in want
He makes us to lie down on the park benches
He leads us beside the still factories
He disturbs our soul
He leads us in the path of destruction for his
*   party's sake*
Yea, though we walk through the valley of
*   Depression*
We anticipate no recovery for those who are with
*   us*
The politicians and diplomats are frightening us
You prepare a reduction of our salary in the
*   presence of our enemies*
Our expenses run over
Surely, poverty and unemployment will follow us
And we will dwell in mortgaged homes forever.

Source B: A comment about the Depression in 1931, by Will Rogers, a famous humorist of the time

We got more corn, more food, more cotton more money in the banks, more everything in the world than any nation ever lived had, yet we are starving to death. We are the first nation in the history of the world to go to the poorhouse in an automobile.

Tasks

1. What can you learn from Source A about attitudes to President Hoover?

2. What message about the Depression is the writer of Source B trying to convey?

Senate
The Upper House of the US Congress (parliament).

Key Term

Hoovervilles

Those Americans who lost their homes moved to the edges of towns and cities and built shacks and shanty towns which became known as 'Hoovervilles' (like the one in Seattle, in the photo on the next page). Hoover was blamed for the lack of support and relief and the sarcastic name for the dwellings soon caught on. It has been estimated that at their peak, several hundred thousand people across the USA lived in Hoovervilles. There were other terms using Hoover's name:

- 'Hoover blankets' were layers of newspapers.
- 'Hoover flags' were men's trouser pockets inside out to show they had no money.

Family life

The Depression had a tremendous impact on family life. Marriages fell from 1.23 million in 1929 to 982,000 in 1932 because young people were reluctant to take on commitments when there were few jobs and little prospect of improvements in the economy. There was an accompanying fall in the birth rate. The suicide rate across the USA increased dramatically, reaching a peak of 17.4 per 100,000 people from a rate of 12.6 in 1926 (look back at Source C on page 18).

In some states, for example Arkansas, schools were closed for ten months in the year because there was not enough money to pay teachers – teachers in Chicago were not paid during the

A Hooverville in Seattle. Why were Hoovervilles such a source of embarrassment for the Republicans?

winter of 1932–33. The magazine *Fortune* estimated that in the autumn of 1932 about 25 per cent of the population was receiving no income. Another estimate was that, of the 3.8 million female one-parent families, only about 20,000 could expect to receive any financial support. In some towns and cities across the USA, where there were not enough soup kitchens and cheap meal centres, people scavenged for food. If there was nothing to scavenge, then they would resort to stealing food.

Source C: From *The Lean Years* by H Miflin, 1960, describing the stealing of food by children

*By 1932, organised looting of food was a nationwide phenomenon. Helen Hall, a Philadelphia social worker, told a **Senate** committee that many families with unemployed parents sent their children out to steal from wholesale markets, to snatch milk from babies and to steal clothes to exchange them for food.*

Source D: From a speech by Congressman G Huddlestone, 1932. He was addressing a Senate Committee about living conditions in the Depression

Any thought that there has been no starvation is utter nonsense. People are actually starving by the thousands today. They are living such a scrambling, precarious existence, and suffering from lack of clothing, food and nourishment, until they are subject to being swept away at any time, and many are now being swept away.

Tasks

3. In what ways was family life affected by the Depression?

4. Use the information and Sources A, B, C and D to write a protest poem about the lack of schooling and food for children in the Depression. Address the poem to the president or the Senate.

Black Americans

When the Depression began, black workers were often the first to be sacked, and their unemployment rate was 50 per cent by 1933. Furthermore, they suffered wage cuts and saw black businesses close down at an alarming rate.

Source E: From *Hard Times* by Studs Terkel, 1970. It is from an interview with Clifford Burke, a black American who lived through the Depression

The Negro was born in depression. The Great Depression as you call it didn't mean much to him. The Depression only became official when it hit the white man.

Source F: From an article 'Negroes out of work', published on 22 April 1931, about the impact of the Depression on black Americans

The percentage of Negroes among the unemployed runs as four, five, six times as their population warrants. When jobs are scarce, preference is given to the white worker in case of a vacancy; but worse than that, a fairly widespread tendency is observed to replace Negro workers with whites. White girls have replaced Negro waiters, hotelworkers and elevator operators.

Tasks

5. What does Source E mean when it says, 'The Depression only became official when it hit the white man?'

6. Look at Sources E and F. What do you learn about the position of black Americans at this time?

Civil unrest

Many ordinary Americans did not meekly accept the hardships of the Depression. Some of those still in employment went on strike because of the reduced wages they had to accept. Sometimes farmers blockaded roads into towns until they received money for their produce.

Source G: From an interview with Ed Paulsen in 1970. Paulsen had been unemployed in San Francisco during the Hoover presidency

We'd say 'let's go to City Hall'. There used to be cops on horseback in those days. Sometimes it got to killing. I think on that day three were killed. We were a gentle crowd. We just wanted to go to work . . . we weren't talking revolution – we were talking jobs.

Source H: From an article in *Time* magazine, October 1931, by W Green – a moderate trade union leader

No social order is secure where wealth flows into the hands of the few away from the many. I warn the people who are exploiting the workers that they can only drive them so far before the workers turn on them and destroy them! The exploiters are taking no account of the history of nations in which governments have been overturned. Revolutions grow out of the depths of hunger.

Tasks

7. What can you learn from Source G about attitudes to demonstrators at this time?

8. Study Sources C and D on the previous page and then read Source H. Why might some members of the Senate be concerned about the reports given in Sources C and D?

An uneven Depression

Though unemployment reached 16 million, there were many in the USA who did not experience hardship in the Depression. Most wealthy people remained rich and some were able to buy land and businesses cheaply at the height of the crisis. Personal spending did fall, but the table below indicates that many people had large disposable incomes.

Year	Personal consumption in $ billions
1929	128.1
1930	120.3
1931	116.6
1932	106.0

Personal consumption, 1929–32.

Source G: From an interview taken by Studs Terkel, an oral historian, in 1970. The interviewee was a psychiatrist in the 1930s

You wouldn't know there was a depression going on . . . don't forget that the highest unemployment was less than 20 per cent. My patients paid reasonable fees – I came across a handbook that I had between 1931 and 1934 and in those days I was making $2,000 a month.

Task

9. *How could Hoover use Source G and the table to convince Americans that the economic crisis was not as severe as generally thought?*

Examination practice

Question 1 – cross-referencing

Does the evidence of Source B support Sources C and D about the impact of the Depression? (The sources are on pages 24–5.)

How to answer

This question is about cross-referencing, question (b) in Paper 2. You will need to analyse Sources B, C and D.

To do this:
- Begin by looking at Source B and working out what it says about the impact.
- Look at Source C and find points of agreement/disagreement with Source B.
- Look at Source D and find points of agreement/disagreement with Source B.
- Then make your judgement – you can do this by beginning a new paragraph. Start with the word . . . 'Overall.' This should ensure you are answering correctly.

Now answer the question, making sure that your answer is clear and direct. It must cover all three sources and above all there must be some judgement within the response. An examiner will be looking for such words and phrases as: 'to a degree', 'to a certain extent', 'completely', 'whereas', 'on the other hand', 'however'.

Who were the Bonus Marchers?

As Hoover became gradually more unpopular, he faced a challenge from an unexpected quarter in 1932. With wages still falling and unemployment still rising, resentment grew and one group, ex-soldiers from the First World War, organised a mass lobbying effort to get aid for themselves and their families.

The government had promised these veterans a bonus for serving in the war, payable in 1945. The veterans felt that they could not wait that long. In May and June 1932, a Bonus Expeditionary Force, made up of over 12,000 unemployed and homeless veterans from all over the USA, marched to Washington DC to voice their support of a bill which would allow early payment of the bonuses. They built a shanty town (called Bonus City) on Anacostia Flats outside the capital and said they would stay there until the bonus bill was passed. Final estimates put the number of men at 22,000, but with wives and children it is thought there were some 40,000.

Washington DC had hardly been affected by the Depression and when the thousands of ragged

> ### Communist
> A believer in the theory that society should be classless, private property abolished, and land and businesses owned collectively. Following the Communist Revolution in Russia in 1917, there had been a growing fear that communism might spread to the USA and destroy the system of government.

Key Term

men and women turned up, government officials labelled them a rabble. This was unjust, because the men organised their Hooverville in a military manner and the protestors were very disciplined.

To pay the bonus would have cost $2.3 billion and Hoover felt that it was simply too much – Congress supported him. Congress did provide money for transport home for the marchers but about 5,000 refused to leave. Some government officials said that **communists** led the Bonus Army. When the police came in to clear them from some of the old buildings they lived in, conflict broke out and two veterans were killed.

The Battle of Anacostia Field

Hoover responded by calling on the army to control the situation. Orders were sent to MacArthur, Army Chief of Staff. He was told to disperse the Bonus Marchers. Cavalry units, tanks, infantry with fixed bayonets and a machine-gun detachment marched on the veterans. The camp at Anacostia was razed. More than 100 people were injured and a baby died of tear gas poisoning in the 'clearance'.

This became known as the Battle of Anacostia Field, and it left a bitter taste in the mouth of many Americans. It seemed to show the gulf between Hoover and the ordinary American people who were suffering so much as a result of the Depression. Some even thought that the USA was on the verge of revolution.

Bonus Marchers setting up their Hooverville, Bonus City, in Washington DC, 1932. Why would another Hooverville be doubly embarrassing for President Hoover?

Source A: From an interview with A E McIntyre, Federal Trade Commissioner, who witnessed the events of 28 July 1932

When the army appeared, the Bonus people started beating on tin pans and shouted 'here come our buddies'. They expected the army to be in sympathy with them ... The 12th Infantry was in full battle dress. Each had a gas mask and his belt was full of tear gas bombs ... Soon almost everybody disappeared from view, because tear gas bombs exploded ... Flames were coming up, where the soldiers had set fire to the buildings in order to drive these people out.

Source B: US historian F L Allen writing in 1932 about the attack on the Bonus Marchers

Suddenly there was chaos, cavalrymen were riding into the crowd, infantrymen were throwing tear gas bombs. A crowd of spectators was pursued by the cavalry. The troops moved on scattering the marchers and home-going government clerks alike ... that evening the Washington sky glowed with fire.

Source C: From an interview with Studs Terkel in 1970. The interviewee was in the Bonus Army and was describing the attack on the Marchers

On 28 July the great MacArthur came down Pennsylvania Avenue. Behind him were tanks and troops of the regular army. When the Bonus guys wouldn't move, the regular army poked them with bayonets and hit them on the head with rifle butts. The soldiers threw tear gas and vomiting gas ... They were younger than the marchers. MacArthur was looked upon as a hero.

Source D: From a US newspaper article of the time, about the incident at Anacostia

What a pitiful spectacle is that of the great American government, mightiest in the world, chasing unarmed men, women and children with army tanks.

Soldiers driving the Bonus Army out of Washington DC with tear gas, July 1932.

Tasks

1. *In groups of three, make a list of reasons why you think Hoover and Congress were unwilling to pay the marchers. Decide what you think are the most important reasons. Feed back your group's work and put forward your conclusions to the class.*

2. *Why do you think that Hoover resorted to force against the Bonus Marchers?*

3. *In groups, role play a discussion about the reaction to the use of force, with each of you playing one of the following parts: the Bonus Marchers, the soldiers in the regular army, the unemployed, the people of Washington.*

4. *Does Source C support Sources A and B about the treatment of the Bonus Marchers? Explain your answer. (Remember the points made on page 27 about answering a cross-referencing question.)*

Why was Roosevelt elected president?

By 1932, many Americans were demanding action. They were tired of ideals like self-reliance and rugged individualism, and talk of prosperity being just around the corner. The ideas of 1928 seemed not to have worked and people wanted change.

Though there had been some federal action, there was a growing call for a bolder approach. Such boldness was being shown in New York State, where Governor Franklin Roosevelt had persuaded the state legislature to spend $20 million on helping the unemployed. It was the first state to take such a step.

In June 1932, Roosevelt accepted the Democratic Party nomination to run for president. In his acceptance speech he said:

'I pledge you, I pledge myself, to a new deal for the American people.'

Were the Republicans responsible for the Depression? While Roosevelt was campaigning to be president, he certainly blamed them. The charges he laid at the Republicans' door in campaign speeches during 1932 are described in Sources A and B. Others seemed to share Roosevelt's opinion of the Republican government, as can be seen from Source C.

So, was it the Republican government and Hoover's unpopularity, rather than Roosevelt's solutions for the Depression, that won him the election? Some historians have suggested this, as shown in Source D and, furthermore, in Source E it seems that Roosevelt's solution was quite vague.

Source A: From an election speech by Roosevelt in Iowa, 1932, describing the failings of the Hoover government

I accuse the present Administration of being the greatest spending Administration during peacetime in all our history. It is an Administration that has piled bureau on bureau, commission on commission and has failed to anticipate the needs and the reduced earning power of the people.

Source B: From an election speech by Roosevelt in 1932. He blamed the Republican government for the Depression

First it encouraged speculation and overproduction through its false economic policies. Second, it attempted to minimise the Crash and misled people as to its gravity. Third, it wrongly charged the cause to other nations of the world. And finally, it refused to recognise and correct the evils at home which it had brought forth; it delayed reform, it forgot reform.

Source C: A journalist writing at the time of the Bonus March, 1932, describing some of the views that were held about Hoover

Never before in this country has a government fallen to so low a place in popular estimation or been so universally an object of cynical contempt. Never before has a president given his name so freely to toilets and offal dumps, or had his face banished from the cinema screen to avoid the hoots and jeers of children.

Source D: From *Depression and the New Deal*, by R Smalley, 1990. He is describing the confidence of Roosevelt

Roosevelt showed confidence. The Democratic candidate's smile and optimism proved far more popular with the electorate than Hoover's grim looks. This difference in presentation was important because in some ways the two candidates seemed to have similar policies.

Source E: From an election speech Roosevelt gave in 1932. He is explaining his openness

If starvation and dire need on the part of any of our citizens make necessary the appropriation of additional funds which would keep the budget out of balance, I shall not hesitate to tell the American people the full truth and ask them to authorise the expenditure of that additional amount.

Hoover's defeat

Hoover stayed in Washington for much of the campaign and when he did make public appearances, he was often booed. On voting day, people threw stink bombs at his car.

The concept map on the right outlines reasons for Hoover's defeat.

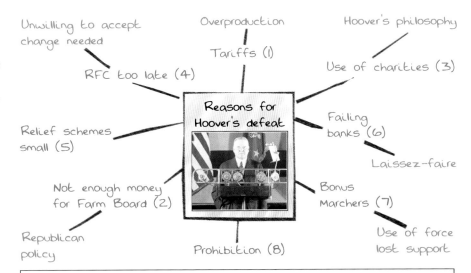

Concept map: **Reasons for Hoover's defeat**
- Unwilling to accept change needed
- Overproduction
- Tariffs (1)
- Hoover's philosophy
- Use of charities (3)
- RFC too late (4)
- Failing banks (6)
- Relief schemes small (5)
- Laissez-faire
- Not enough money for Farm Board (2)
- Bonus Marchers (7)
- Republican policy
- Prohibition (8)
- Use of force lost support

NOTES
1. Hawley-Smoot tariff kept custom duties high on imports. This reduced exports, but industry continued to produce goods.
2. Farm Board did not help all farmers with their debts and caused some resentment.
3. Reliance on charities for help with the unemployed – Hoover naïve in thinking this would solve huge scale problems.
4. RFC introduced too late to make an immediate impact.
5. Relief and government schemes were too small in scope.
6. Banks and businesses continued to fail and confidence fell away.
7. Treatment of the Bonus Marchers caused many to drift away from Hoover.
8. Impact of prohibition on farmers and the increase in crime lost Hoover more support.

Roosevelt as governor

Roosevelt was the governor of New York State in the years 1929–33 and thus had to deal with the Crash and Depression as a crucial part of his position. He was keen to ensure that the state legislature played an active part in helping its citizens. He set up a special committee to explore ways to challenge the problems and sought help from all those involved, such as business people, trade unionists and economists.

Source F: From a speech by Roosevelt in 1931 (Roosevelt was the governor of the state of New York at the time), describing his views on the role of government

One of the duties of the government is that of caring for those of its citizens who find themselves the victims of such adverse circumstances as makes them unable to obtain even the necessities for mere existence without the aid of others. That responsibility is recognised by every civilised nation ... To these unfortunate citizens aid must be extended by government, not as a matter of charity, but as a matter of social duty.

Tasks

1. *Why is Roosevelt so critical of Hoover and his administration in Sources A and B (page 30)?*

2. *Study Sources C and D (page 30). Why does Roosevelt seem an appealing choice to the voters?*

3. *In what ways could Hoover claim to have tackled the Depression successfully?*

4. *After reading the information on pages 30–32 construct a concept map, like the one above, to show why Roosevelt won the 1932 presidential election. Use the sources to focus on the positive side of Roosevelt. Do not use the points about Hoover in the map on this page.*

5. *Design two posters for the 1932 presidential campaign – one for Hoover and one for Roosevelt.*

6. *Having read the following page, what can you learn from the result of the election about the nature of Roosevelt's victory?*

Roosevelt's campaign

Source G: From Roosevelt's biography by A P Hatch. Here, Hatch is describing part of Roosevelt's campaign tour

They waited for him in stadiums at fair grounds and on little station platforms – and he hastened happily to greet them. Roosevelt made about twenty speeches a day and made a thousand friends every day. Each time the train stopped he went out on the rear platform for a word and a joke with the cheering crowd.

Source H: Frances Perkins, Roosevelt's Secretary for Labour after 1933, writing in 1946 about the 1932 campaign

In the campaign, Roosevelt saw thousands of Americans. He liked going around the country. His personal relationship with the crowds was on a warm simple level of friendly neighbourly exchange of affection.

Source I: Democratic election poster, 1932

What does this suggest about Republican attitudes to the Depression?

Source J: From a speech Roosevelt made during the presidential campaign, outlining his solutions if he were elected

Our greatest primary task is to put people to work. This is no unsolvable problem if we face it wisely and courageously. It can be accomplished in part by the government itself, treating the task as if it were a war, but at the same time, through its employment, accomplishing greatly needed projects to stimulate and reorganise the use of natural resources.

Everywhere he went, Roosevelt knew that he had to create a mood of optimism. The despair that many felt was becoming ingrained and he was keen to let people know that he understood their feelings and he would break the cycle of despondency. Roosevelt won the election by a landslide – only six of the forty-eight states voted for Hoover. The result was: Hoover = 15,759,000 votes, Roosevelt = 22,810,000 votes.

Roosevelt was able to seize on those issues that Hoover had found almost impossible to solve. He offered a vision and put forward a number of easily understood policies:

- Creation of jobs
- Assistance for unemployed and the poor (relief)
- Government to help both agriculture and industry
- Protection against harsh employers.

Examination practice

1. What can you learn from Source F (page 31) about Roosevelt's view of the role of government? (4 marks)
2. Does the evidence of Source H support Source G and Source D about support for Roosevelt? (6 marks)
3. How useful are Sources I and J as evidence of the 1932 presidential campaign? (Read page 51 in Chapter 4 to look at the approach for this type of question.) (8 marks)
4. 'Roosevelt was elected president in 1932 because of his optimism and confidence.' Use the sources and your own knowledge to say whether you agree with this. (Read pages 62–63 in Chapter 5 to examine the approach to this type of question.) (12 marks)

3 Attempts at recovery: the New Deal

Source A

From President Roosevelt's inaugural speech, March 1933

This is the time to speak the truth, the whole truth, frankly and boldly. Nor need we shrink from honestly facing conditions in our country today. This great nation will endure as it has endured, will revive and prosper. So first of all let me assert my firm belief that the only thing we have to fear is fear itself. Only a fool will deny the dark realities of the moment … This country asks for action and action now!

Task

What can you learn from Source A about Roosevelt's attitude to solving the USA's problems?

Roosevelt introduced a series of proposals which tackled the problems of the Depression in a way that was, for the USA, quite revolutionary. For the first time, the federal government began to take responsibility for its citizens – the USA had to accept that it would only emerge from its troubles if *laissez-faire* and 'rugged individualism' were abandoned.

By the end of this chapter, you will be able to answer the following questions:

• What were the aims and objectives of the New Deal?
• What were the one hundred days and why were they important?
• In what ways did the New Deal tackle the problems in unemployment agriculture, and industry?
• Why was the Tennessee Valley Authority important in the New Deal?
• What was the dust bowl and what effect did it have?
• What was the Second New Deal?

Source skills

You will cover inference and cross-referencing questions from Paper 2. At the end there will be the chance to answer an interpretation question – there is further advice about answering this type of question in Chapter 4.

What were the aims of the New Deal?

Biography Franklin Delano Roosevelt, 1882–1945

1905	Married Eleanor Roosevelt (she was a distant cousin of FDR)
1911–13	**Democrat** member of New York state legislature
1913–20	Assistant Secretary of the navy
1920	Nominated Democratic vice-presidential candidate
1921	Suffered an attack of polio which left him unable to walk properly
1929–33	Governor of New York State
1933–45	President of the USA

In his nomination speech to the Democratic Party, Roosevelt had promised the American people a 'new deal', and now that he was president it was time to introduce it. He felt it was his task to restore the faith that most Americans had lost in their country. Roosevelt was an experimenter at heart and above all he was receptive to new ideas. He employed Republicans as well as Democrats, **conservatives** as well as **liberals**, university intellectuals as well as experienced politicians. The aims of the New Deal are set out in the table below.

Relief	• Assist in the removal of poverty • Provide food for the starving • Intervene to prevent people from losing homes/farms
Recovery	• Ensure that the economy was boosted so that people could be given jobs
Reform	• Ensure that there were welfare provisions in the future to help the unemployed, old, sick, disabled and the destitute.

The aims of the New Deal.

Source A: From *History of the USA* by H Brogan, 1985, describing the impact of Roosevelt's inaugural speech

The inaugural speech was one of the turning points of American history. In a few minutes Roosevelt did what had so wearyingly eluded Hoover for four years: he gave back to his countrymen their hope and energy. By the end of the week half a million letters – (nearly all of them favourable) had poured into the White House.

Source B: A cartoon from March 1933: Roosevelt taking over from Hoover at the White House

A mural entitled *The New Deal*, **painted by Albrizio in 1934 and dedicated to President Roosevelt**

Notice the figure of Roosevelt in the centre, behind a despairing worker, and surrounded by different kinds of workers.

The economic theory put forward by Roosevelt

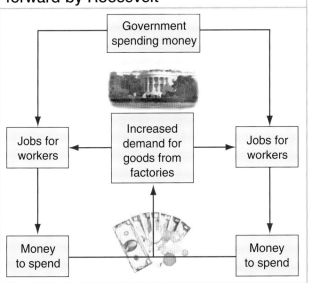

Government spending money

Jobs for workers

Increased demand for goods from factories

Jobs for workers

Money to spend

Money to spend

Tasks

1. *Study Sources B and C. Why should some Americans be surprised at the drawings of Roosevelt? (The biography box will help you.)*

2. *What can you learn from Sources B and C about Roosevelt's approach to the problems facing the USA?*

3. *What is the artist's attitude to Roosevelt in Source C?*

4. *Look at Source D. How was Roosevelt's approach to the economy different to Hoover's? Explain your answer.*

5. *Imagine you are* **governor** *of a state which has industrial and agricultural workers. Write a letter to President Roosevelt indicating why his proposed solutions to the Depression will help these people.*

What were the 100 days?

After his inauguration, Roosevelt set to work immediately. He attacked the problems of the Great Depression and pushed through a huge number of government programmes. The programmes aimed to restore the shattered economy and Congress met from March 9 until 16 June 1933. This period became known as the 100 days. During this time Roosevelt also ended prohibition. On 12 March 1933, he joked 'I think this would be a good time for a beer.'

The table below shows the key features of the activities of Roosevelt's 100 days setting up the **Alphabet Agencies**.

Key Terms

Alphabet Agencies
Those bodies set up in the New Deal to tackle the problems of the Depression. They were abbreviated and were known by the letters of the alphabet, for example the Civilian Conservation Corps was the CCC.

Fireside chat
When Roosevelt spoke to the nation it was assumed that people sat by the fire as they listened to him. The image was of a cosy friendly chat.

Emergency Banking Act (EBA)	To restore confidence in the banking system. Part of the Act prevented banks from investing savings deposits in the stock market which was too unpredictable to guarantee the safety of those funds.
Federal Emergency Relief Administration (FERA)	Emergency relief and funds of $500 million were provided for the unemployed. It was a temporary measure because Roosevelt did not want his opponents to think the government was just handing money out to the unemployed.
Civilian Conservation Corps (CCC)	Designed to tackle unemployment: men between the ages of 18–25 were offered work in conservation projects. The workers planted trees, to prevent soil erosion. By the start of the war, more than two million men had been granted some work with the CCC.
National Recovery Administration (NRA)	This agency was to set fair prices, wages and working conditions. Participants displayed the Blue Eagle emblem. The Act which established the NRA was removed by the **Supreme Court** in 1935 (see page 39).
Tennessee Valley Authority (TVA)	A huge area covering several states was to be singled out and re-developed. The Tennessee Valley was a poor, backward area which had suffered erosion and flooding. The aim was to resolve these problems and create a prosperous agricultural area.
Home Owner's Loan Act and Home Owner's Loan Corporation (HOLC)	This provided low interest loans to assist mortgage repayments.
Agricultural Adjustment Act (AAA)	Aimed to increase farm prices and in some cases did so by ploughing up crops and slaughtering animals (see page 40). Prices did rise slowly. The Supreme Court rejected the Act in 1936.
Farm Credit Administration (FCA)	Money was made available to assist farmers with their mortgages and this saved many from eviction. Twenty per cent of farmers benefited from the scheme.
Public Works Administration (PWA)	Monies were made available for huge-scale public works. $3,300 million was spent by this agency.
Reconstruction Finance Corporation (RFC)	Hoover's agency was retained (see page 23) but Roosevelt pumped in more money. Banks and businesses were able to use some of the $15 billion pumped in by Roosevelt to begin once again the process of investment.

The most important task waiting for Roosevelt was stemming the crisis in banking. More than 2,000 banks had closed in the twelve months before he had become president and if there was to be any confidence in the banking and commercial sectors, people had to feel that they could save and invest without fear of huge financial losses.

Furthermore, those who were saving in banks were withdrawing money at an alarming rate, thus undermining the whole banking system. Roosevelt closed all banks for ten days and then, on the radio (60 million people listened to him), explained his plans – he would allow those banks with assets to re-open and those without would be closed until he and his advisers put forward a rescue programme. He assured people that money was safer in a bank than at home. When the banks re-opened, people no longer wished to withdraw their savings and many put back what had recently been withdrawn. Roosevelt had brought back confidence in the system.

His radio talk became the first of many 'fireside chats' (see Sources A, B and C).

A MAN TALKING TO HIS FRIENDS

Source B: From *The Roosevelt I Knew* by Frances Perkins, 1946

When he broadcast I realised how clearly his mind focused on the people listening at the other end. As he talked his head would nod and his hands would move in simple, natural, comfortable gestures. His face would smile and light up as though he were actually sitting on the front porch or in the kitchen with them. People felt this and it bound them to him in affection.

Source C: From *The New Deal* by H Brogan, 1968, describing the impression Roosevelt made on people

In his fireside chats on the radio, he projected himself and his message into millions of homes. Most years he made extensive tours and hundreds of thousands saw for themselves that big smile, the jauntily cocked cigarette holder, glasses and jutting jaw made famous by photographs and cartoons.

Tasks

1. What was the intention of the activity of the 100 days?

2. Look at sources A, B and C. Why do you think the 'fireside chats' were so effective for Roosevelt?

3. Look at the table describing the key activities of the 100 days. Make a table that divides the activities into three groups, as below, and decide in which column the activities should be placed. If you need to, look at the table on page 34 about the three aims of relief, recovery and reform. What do you notice about your decisions?

Relief	Recovery	Reform

How did the New Deal tackle unemployment, industry and agriculture?

Unemployment

Roosevelt asked Congress for legislation to help the unemployed. He wanted legislation that would involve government in direct relief, provide money for public works projects such as roads, dams, schools, etc. and set up various programmes to put as many young unemployed people to work as possible.

The CCC

The Civilian Conservation Corps was set up to create jobs for the many men who were hobos or lived in Hoovervilles. Among the first recruits were several thousand members of the Bonus Army. CCC workers received food, clothing and one dollar per day. This scheme was quite popular as Source A describes. By August 1933 there were about 250,000 working on the CCC.

Workers in the Civilian Conservation Corps. Can you suggest reasons why some Americans criticised the CCC?

Source A: From *Newsweek* magazine, 8 April 1933, describing the intent of the CCC

A new army of pioneers will go into the woods within a few weeks. Across 150,000,000 acres of forest lands ... will march an army of workers who are at the moment unemployed and trudging the streets. It is clear that this army will be fully enlisted because applications have rained into Washington from all over the country.

Federal Emergency Relief Act (FERA)

FERA was authorised to distribute $500 million through grants to state and local agencies for relief. Neither Congress nor the people really liked the idea of Americans being given money by the government or states and as a result, on 8 November, Congress passed legislation forming the Civil Works Administration to create public jobs. FERA was led by Harry Hopkins, an experienced administrator and social worker.

Civil Works Administration (CWA)

By January 1934, about four million Americans, mostly unskilled workers, were on the CWA's payroll. The Works Project Administration replaced the CWA in 1935, and over the years it employed more than eight million people. Some of the workers built roads, but on occasions this agency was laughed at for creating jobs such as scaring birds away from buildings or sweeping leaves in parks.

	Unemployed in millions	Percentage of workforce unemployed
1933	12.8	24.9
1934	11.3	21.7
1935	10.6	20.1

Unemployment, 1933–35.

Industry

Roosevelt was determined to increase the productivity of American industry, and to help industry recover, the National Industry Recovery Act (NIRA) was passed.

Source B: A cartoon published in a newspaper in 1933: 'The Spirit of the New Deal'.

Why could Roosevelt's supporters claim that the New Deal was a success for industry?

The National Industrial Recovery Act

Part of the NIRA was the National Recovery Administration (NRA). This sought to have employers draw up common codes of employment such as maximum hours and **minimum wages**. In the 1920s some groups of employers had got together to fix wages/prices and it was hoped that these codes would end the fierce competition which had resulted in wage levels being reduced.

To encourage business leaders to comply with the codes, the NRA launched a publicity campaign – it adopted as its symbol a blue eagle poster and asked people to buy only goods from businesses displaying the poster. The people did rally to this call and the symbol of the blue eagle (see Source B) appeared all over the country.

Source C: From A New Jersey factory notice board, 1933, showing workers what needed to be done to stimulate the economy

President Roosevelt has done his part; now you do something. Buy something – buy anything, paint your kitchen, send a telegram, give a party, get a car, pay a bill, rent a flat, fix your roof, build a house … It doesn't matter what you do – but get going and keep going. This old world is starting to move.

Source D: From one of Roosevelt's fireside chats, June 1933. He was talking about employers paying fair wages

If all employers in each competitive group agree to pay their workers the same reasonable wages – and require the same hours – reasonable hours – then higher wages will hurt no employer. Such action is better for the employer than unemployment and low wages, because it makes more buyers for his product. That is the simple idea which is at the very heart of the Industrial Recovery Act.

Tasks

1. Study the table on unemployment on page 38. What conclusions can be drawn about the New Deal in its first two years of operation?

2. Why do you think that members of the Bonus Army were amongst the first recruits to the CCC?

3. Study Source A. What can you learn form Source A about the setting up of the CCC? (Remember what was said about inferences on page 20.)

4. Look at the information and photo on page 38 and sources A and B. Do you think Roosevelt was successful in achieving his New Deal aims on unemployment? Draw up a balance sheet – on one side have success and on the other failure. Explain your points carefully.

5. What can you learn from Source B about the New Deal?

6. Does Source D support the evidence of Sources B and C about how to solve the problems facing US industry? (Remember, this is a cross-reference question. Look at Chapter 2 page 27 to go over the approach to this.)

Source E: Earnings and prices in the USA, 1920–41. The year 1926 is taken as the base line

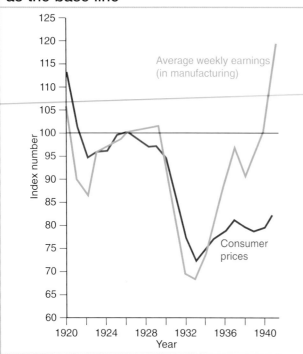

Source F: Cotton being ploughed back into the ground

- Though many hungry people did not understand the logic of destroying animals and not using them, farmers were generally satisfied with the policy because prices did begin to rise.
- By 1936, incomes were one and a half times higher than they had been in 1933.

Source G: From *FDR and the New Deal*, by W Leuchtenberg, an American historian writing in 1963, describing one effect of the AAA

The AAA decided to prevent a glut by slaughtering over six million pigs and two hundred thousand cows ... many piglets overran the stockyard and scampered through the streets of Chicago ... the country was horrified.

Agriculture

Roosevelt was aware that farmers had experienced several years of low prices and poor profits. He was keen to introduce measures which would have an immediate effect and ensure that farmers would be able to carry out their work without making losses. Consequently, the Farm Credit Administration and Agricultural Administration were introduced.

The Farm Credit Administration (FCA)

- Twenty per cent of farmers used the funds offered by government.
- Low interest loans were made readily available to farmers to help them pay of their debts.

The Agricultural Adjustment Act (AAA)

This proved to be rather controversial. It was set up to increase farmers' incomes but it was decided that to achieve this, production levels would have to drop. As production fell, then prices would rise and farmers could begin to recover. Farmers would be paid by the government to grow less.

- More than five million pigs were killed, and thousands of hectares of cotton were ploughed back into the ground.

Tasks

7. *What can you learn about the New Deal from Source E? Explain your answer. (Remember that in an inference question you are expected to make a judgement. Above all, you should not copy out the source. When using a graph look for such things as quick/slow increases, increases which double or treble, or inconsistencies.)*

8. *Look at the Sources F and G. Explain why many people at this time were horrified by the killing of large numbers of animals and the ploughing back of crops.*

9. *Was Roosevelt a friend to the farmers? Explain your answer.*

Why was the TVA important?

Source A: From *TVA: Adventure in Planning* by J Huxley, 1943. Huxley had surveyed the Tennessee Valley in the early 1930s

The erosion was appalling. Here before me, was the basic productivity of an area being stripped from a vast region and being taken to the sea by the river. I saw outcrops of bare rock which three generations ago had been covered with rich soil over a metre in depth. The amount of soil annually washed or blown out of the USA is estimated at three million tons.

Study Source A. What can you learn about the problems that farmers faced in the Tennessee Valley area?

Socialist state

A state in which the government, not private individuals, controls the means of production.

One of the most important features of the New Deal was the establishment of the Tennessee Valley Authority (TVA). The Tennessee Valley was one of the most depressed regions of the USA. More than half the population of 2.5 million were receiving relief and few people had electricity. Annual flood damage (the result of erosion caused by de-forestation) was put at $1.75 million.

Hence, if this area could be re-invigorated then Roosevelt could show that his policies were clearly aimed at benefiting the country. Furthermore, it was hoped that immediate improvements could be made in the area. The TVA was to be an independent public body which would have control of government property at Muscle Shoals, Tennessee.

The scope of the TVA was immense and it aimed not only to regenerate the region but also to create jobs. It was to be responsible for generating and distributing electric power for that area by means of the creation of a system of dams which would enable flood control. The many dams meant there would be reservoirs, power plants and it was hoped that with cheap electricity and an end to flooding, industry would be attracted to the area.

The Norris Dam, one of thirty TVA sites. This was part of a network which helped generate electricity for the TVA.

The success of the TVA

The Authority would also develop river navigation and the manufacture and distribution of fertiliser to farmers in order to re-establish the area. The TVA had the power to build recreation areas, as well as to provide health and welfare facilities. Eventually, the activities of the TVA covered seven states, 40,000 square miles (see map) with a population of seven million people and did prove to be one of the successes of the New Deal.

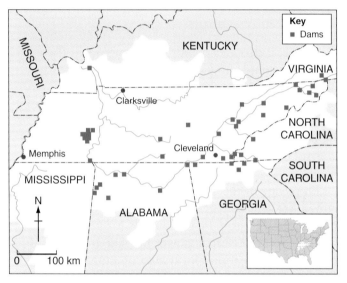

Map of the Tennessee Valley area.

These photographs are before and after shots of an area in Tennessee Valley, where the planting of trees successfully halted land erosion.

Opposition to the TVA

The TVA was not received well by everyone – farmers whose land was flooded were of course opponents, as were some big business owners who felt that the USA was moving towards becoming a **socialist state**. These business people campaigned against other areas of the USA being given similar treatment to the Tennessee Valley.

The TVA is still in existence today.

Tasks

1. *Write a 'fireside chat' speech for President Roosevelt (see pages 36–37) that informs people why he is introducing the TVA scheme.*

2. *Write a speech for some business people showing why the TVA is a sign that President Roosevelt is taking the USA down the road to a socialist state and why it should be opposed.*

3. *Draw a concept map about the TVA like the one below. On the first layer, insert the reasons for setting up the TVA. On the second layer, insert the solutions to the problems. Put the reasons in one colour and the solutions in another. This will help you to see whether you have completed the task correctly.*

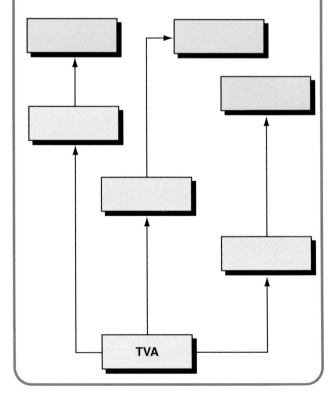

What was the dust bowl?

Task

1. *What can you learn from Source A about the impact of the climate on farmers?*

Farm machinery buried after a dust storm, 1936.

Not only did farmers have to face the economic problems of the 1920s and the Depression, but they also experienced severe drought in the years 1932 to 1936. The worst hit were parts of Texas, Oklahoma, Colorado, New Mexico and Kansas. Poor farming methods exhausted the soil, the soil turned to dust and when the wind came there were dust storms – the effects of the storms can be seen in the photograph above. The areas became known as the 'dust bowl' (see Source A).

> **Source A: From the *Crash to the Blitz* by R Cabell-Philips, 1969, describing the impact of the weather on parts of the USA**
>
> *In the years 1934–38 prolonged drought dried up millions of acres of farmland and pasturage. Dust storms of unprecedented violence darkened the skies from Texas to New York. Floods, hurricanes and tornadoes spread havoc throughout the mid-West. Floods and windstorms during that period killed 3,678 and injured 18,791 and damaged more than 500,000 buildings.*

Migration

These issues forced about one million people to leave their homes and seek work in the fruit-growing areas of the west coast. The farmers and their families packed what they could, tied it to their car and set off for the west. Those from Oklahoma were nicknamed 'Okies' and those from Arkansas were 'Arkies'. The terms quickly became derogatory because the people were seen as threatening – as hobos and possible criminals. The plight of these people has been captured in the photographs of Dorothea Lange (see Sources B and C on the next page) and the novel *The Grapes of Wrath* by John Steinbeck (see Source D also on page 44). Steinbeck's novel and the subsequent film are highly recommended.

The decision to move west

The decision to leave the dust bowl and move west was not taken lightly, for it meant giving up everything. Yet, farmers in the west were quite happy to employ the Okies and the Arkies, simply because they would work for very low wages. They would set up camps at the edge of towns and seek work wherever possible. Naturally, locals did not like them – they were taking their jobs – and so the police were frequently called in to move the unwanted campers away.

Attempts at recovery: the New Deal

Later, Roosevelt established the Farm Security and Resettlement Administration to tackle these farming issues. 650,000 families were given money by the Resettlement Administration, but for many the intervention was rather late.

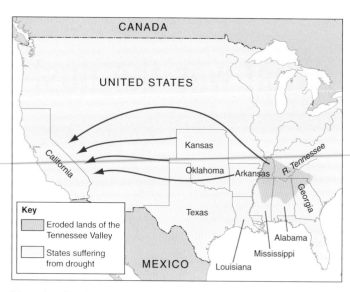

Map showing internal migration in the 1930s.

Source C: From the memoir of Dorothea Lange, *The Assignment I'll Never Forget*, 1960. Here she is describing meeting one of the migrant workers who has arrived in California – see Source B

I approached the hungry woman ... She told me she was 32. She said she had been living on frozen vegetables from surrounding fields and birds that her children had killed. She had just sold the tyres from the car to buy food.

Source D: From *The Grapes of Wrath*, a novel by John Steinbeck, 1939

California's a nice country. But she was stole a long time ago. You never will have seen such pretty country. And you'll pass land which is fine and flat with good water supplies and land that's not being used. You go on that land and you plant a little corn and you'll go to jail. You never been called 'Okie'? ... Well 'Okie' used to mean you were from Oklahoma. Now it means you're a dirty son of a bitch. 'Okie' means you're scum. I hear there's 300,000 of our people there and living like pigs, because everything in California is owned.

Examination practice

In the two following questions you are asked to look at how useful a source can be. There are some detailed explanations on how to answer this type of question (a utility question) in Chapter 4, page 51. Here you can begin to consider the usefulness of a source by:

- looking at what type of source it is (e.g. a photograph, a novel)
- what the source says and whether it is accurate
- what the purpose of the source was.

Try to look for positive points as well as limitations for the source. Do remember that all sources have some use.

Now have a go yourself

1. Look at Sources B and C. Lange was employed by the government. Does this mean that these two sources are of no use to the person studying the New Deal? Explain your answer. (8 marks)

2. Study Source D. This is from a novel about the 1930s. What limitations does this source have to someone studying the USA in the 1930s? (8 marks)

What was the second New Deal?

Source A: From 'The New Deal in review, 1936–40' in *New Republic*, a US magazine, May 1940, describing the work of the New Deal

The New Deal has done far more for the general welfare of the country and its citizens than any administration in the previous history of the nation. Its relief for the underprivileged in city and country has been indispensable. Without this relief an appalling amount of misery would have resulted ... the New Deal has accomplished much of permanent benefit to the nation.

Do you agree that the New Deal 'accomplished much of permanent benefit'?

The New Deal continued into 1934, and Roosevelt received criticism for not doing enough to reduce unemployment, and criticism for doing too much and increasing the role of government (see Chapter 4). There were still about 10 million unemployed and he was aware that he would have to show some successes with the presidential elections approaching. In January 1935, in his annual message to Congress, Roosevelt introduced his second New Deal, a broad programme of reform to help farmers, workers, the poor and the unemployed.

The Works Progress Administration (WPA)

The WPA was a scheme headed by Harry Hopkins, who had been in charge of FERA (see page 38) and he was quick to put the programme into action. The mainstay of the programme was funding and building projects, including hospitals, schools, airports, harbours, etc. thus creating employment. Its other responsibilities included:

- overseeing a $4.8 billion relief programme
- putting unemployed teachers back to work by creating the Adult Education Programme
- creating community service schemes to employ artists, writers and actors.

Key Terms

Collective bargaining
Negotiation of workers, represented by union leaders, with employers.

Interstate commerce
Trade between two or more states.

Recession
A period of declining productivity and reduced economic activity.

Both directly and indirectly the WPA improved the quality of life in communities across the USA. In all, during its five years of operation, it gave work to more than eight million people and spent $11 billion. Roosevelt described the work of the WPA as 'priming the pump' – in other words, the government was acting by re-starting the economic machinery.

National Labour Relations Act

Roosevelt was keen to protect the rights of workers, and when the NIRA was removed in 1935 he sought another approach. In the same year he was able to bring in the Wagner Act or National Labour Relations Act:

- The Act upheld the right of workers to organise and enter into **collective bargaining**. In 1933, there were three million trade union members and in 1939, more than nine million.
- The Wagner Act set up the National Labour Relations Board which was given power to act against employers who used unfair practices, such as sacking workers who had joined a union.

The business community opposed the Wagner Act and complained that it had defined unfair practices for employers, but not for workers.

Fair Labour Standards Act

Further improvements came with the Fair Labour Standards Act in 1938. By this Act:

- Minimum wages and maximum hours were established for all employees of businesses engaged in **interstate commerce**.
- 300,000 secured higher wages as a result and more than one million had a shorter working week.
- Child labour was not permitted except on farms.

Social Security Act

Perhaps the most important reform was the Social Security Act of 1935. By this Act, the government at last accepted its direct responsibility for meeting the basic needs of its citizens. The Act:

- Established pension benefits for the elderly, the orphaned and those injured in industrial accidents. Pensions were for those over 65, and the funding would be met by a tax on employers and workers.
- Established unemployment benefits which would be funded by a tax on the payrolls of employers.
- Set up the Social Security Board to administer payments.

Some of Roosevelt's critics said that the act did not go far enough, mainly because the benefits were too small. However, there were critics who said the act would ruin the USA because it would discourage people from saving and using their initiative, and make them depend on the government for handouts.

Tasks

1. Study Source B.

- What do you think the cartoonist meant by the phrase 'You remembered me'?

- What can you learn about the role of Roosevelt from this Source?

2. Explain why the Social Security Act is such a significant piece of legislation in US history.

Source B: A cartoon drawn in 1933, called 'You remembered me'. Roosevelt is shown shaking hands with 'The Forgotten Man'

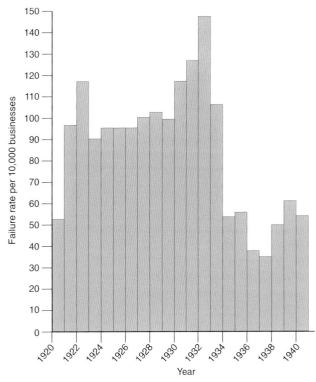

Graph showing business failures, 1920–40.

Reforming Acts

Equally significant were the reforming acts which restricted the activities of banks. Following the Emergency Banking Act, further changes were made. Amongst the most important measures were the Securities Act and the Banking Act. The Securities Act was designed to eliminate fraud in the stock market. Under this law, a company which deliberately deceived investors about its financial status could be sued. The Banking Act prohibited banks from investing savings in the stock market which was too unpredictable to assure the safety of these funds.

Source D: From *The USA since the First World War* by C P Hill, 1967, describing the achievements of the New Deal

The New Deal brought a revolution in the thinking of the American people about the place of the federal government in their lives. The reforms have remained part of the way of the American way of life. Roosevelt gave new heart and vigour to his fellow countrymen just in time to face the trial of the Second World War.

Task

3. *Does Source D support the evidence of Sources B and C about Roosevelt, the New Deal, and the ordinary US citizen?*

   (This is a cross-referencing question – look back at Chapter 2, page 27, to see the approach to this type of question. Remember that a judgement is required based on an analysis of all three sources.)

Achievements

The New Deal had notable positive achievements to its credit: the transformation of the Tennessee Valley, the PWA and the WPA. But far more significant was the simple fact that the New Deal restored hope to millions of men and women by providing them with a job or saving their home.

By 1937, Roosevelt had won a second term and there was a reduction in the pieces of legislation emerging from Congress. However, 1937 and 1938 saw the USA experience another period of **recession**. Roosevelt had decided to cut back on government spending in these years, but he changed his mind, and in June 1938 Congress passed another huge spending bill. Unemployment did fall after 1939 (the year when Roosevelt said the New Deal was at an end), but it did not return to pre-1929 levels until the USA was involved in the Second World War.

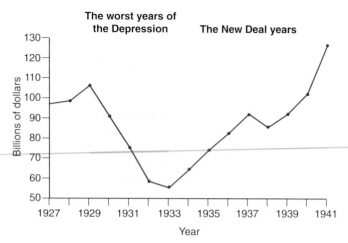

Graph showing the Gross National Product (GNP) in the USA, 1927–41. GNP is the total value of all goods and services produced in a country in one year.

Tasks

4. *Draw a poster to advertise the start of the second New Deal.*

5. *'Roosevelt was successful with the second New Deal.'*
Use the information on pages 45–48, including the sources and graphs, and your own knowledge, to say if you agree with this view.

6. *Re-read the whole chapter (pages 33–48) and then make a concept map of how Roosevelt tried to tackle the problems of the Depression. Put 'Depression' as the central box, and then have arrows leading out on which you write the problems. Then draw a box at the end of each arrow which explains how that problem was solved.*

4 Opposition to the New Deal

Source A 'Ring Around a Roosevelt, Pockets Full of Dough': a cartoonist's view of the New Deal. From the *Washington Post*, May 1938

Tasks

Study Source A.

1. What message is the cartoonist trying to put across about the New Deal?

2. How does the cartoonist get across this message?

3. Do you think this cartoon is useful in studying attitudes to the New Deal? Give at least one reason for your answer.

The New Deal was not popular with all citizens of the USA; indeed there was opposition from a number of individuals and groups. Why did the following groups oppose the New Deal:

- Republicans
- businessmen
- Democrats
- individuals such as Huey Long, Dr Francis Townsend and Father Charles Coughlin
- the Supreme Court?

In this chapter you will find out the answers to this question and examine more closely the nature and extent of this opposition. For example, some opponents, such as Republicans and businessmen, believed Roosevelt was doing too much. Others, for example Huey Long, believed that he was not doing enough.

Source skills

In this chapter we are going to look at the next type of source question you will have to answer in Paper 2 – the **utility** (usefulness) of two sources.

Why did some politicians oppose the New Deal?

Opposition from Republicans and businessmen

The Republicans were strong opponents of the New Deal. Not only were they traditional opponents of the Democrats, they were also the party which represented the interests of America's rich families and large business corporations. These believed that Roosevelt was doing too much to help people and was changing the accepted role of government in the USA.

The American Liberty League

This was set up in 1934 to preserve individual freedom and was backed by wealthy businessmen, two of whom, Alfred Smith and John Davis, rather surprisingly, had previously stood as Democrat presidential candidates.

Key Terms

Conservative Democrats
Democrats who did not want much change.

Thrifty
Careful with spending.

Opposition from Democrats

Even some members of Roosevelt's own party, the Democrats, opposed the New Deal. They were known as **Conservative Democrats**, many of whom came from the South and represented farming areas. They were especially against the Wagner Act (see page 45) which had given greater powers to the trade unions.

A cartoon from the *Philadelphia Enquirer*, 1936. What message is the cartoonist trying to get across?

Task

On the right is a concept map showing some of the reasons for the opposition of Republicans and many businessmen to the New Deal. However, some boxes are not completed.

- *Copy the concept map.*

- *See if you can find other reasons for opposition from these groups. You may get clues from Chapter 3 (pages 33–48).*

- *Complete the blank boxes.*

- *Add extra boxes if you find even more reasons.*

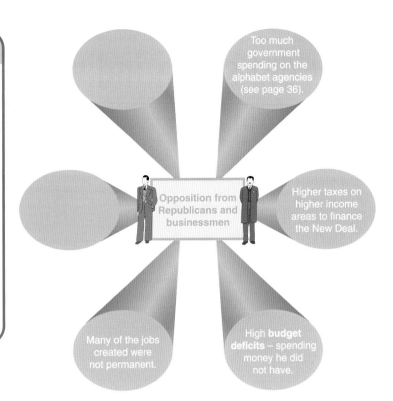

Too much government spending on the alphabet agencies (see page 36).

Opposition from Republicans and businessmen

Higher taxes on higher income areas to finance the New Deal.

Many of the jobs created were not permanent.

High **budget deficits** – spending money he did not have.

Examination practice

The third question of Paper 2 asks you to decide the utility (usefulness) of two sources. This is worth eight marks. The best answers explain the utility and limitations of each source in terms of:

- The content – what the sources show or say, what views they have about the event. This can get you to the top of Level 2, which is 6 marks.
- NOP – the nature, origin and purpose of each source. You must analyse these aspects to reach Level 3 (8 marks).

Here you will concentrate on content. On pages 56–57 we will look at NOP.

Source A: From a speech by a Republican in 1935, criticising the effects of the New Deal

*The New Deal is nothing more or less than an effort to take away from the **thrifty** what the thrifty and their ancestors have accumulated, or may accumulate, and give it to others who have not earned it and never will earn it. Thus, indirectly, it destroys the incentive for all future accumulation. Such a purpose is in defiance of all the ideas upon which our country has been founded.*

Question 1 – source utility

How useful is Source A as evidence of the effects of the New Deal?   (8 marks)

How to answer
- What can you learn from Source A about the effects of the New Deal? (Remember your inference skills, see page 20).
- What is useful about the content of the source? To help you, think about the following questions:
  - What effects does it mention?
  - What view is given about the New Deal? Do you think this was a popular view of the time, i.e. typical of the time?
- Are there any limitations to the content? For example:
  - Does it give a very limited and/or one-sided view?
- What does it *not* tell us about the New Deal?

Why did some individuals oppose the New Deal?

The New Deal also attracted opposition from individuals who believed that Roosevelt was not doing enough. They had their own ideas about what he should be doing. The three most important were:

• Governor Huey Long
• Father Charles Coughlin
• Dr Francis Townsend

Who were they, what ideas did they have and why did they oppose the New Deal?

Huey Long

CONFIDENTIAL

NAME: Huey Long, 1893-1935

Huey Long had been Govenor of the State of Louisiana, ruling it almost as a dictator. Nevertheless, he had shown genuine concern for the state's poor. He taxed the wealthy, especially the oil companies, to pay for improvements such as new bridges across rivers, roads across swamps and new schools. In other words, he had a track record of helping the less privileged.

Long claimed that Roosevelt had failed to share out the nation's wealth fairly and he announced his own plans to do this under the slogan 'Share Our Wealth'. Long said that Roosevelt should confiscate the 'swollen fortunes' of the wealthy and use this to give every American family a house, a car and two or three thousand dollars a year.

He promised to make 'every man a king' and attracted the support of millions of the poor. Membership of 'Share Our Wealth' clubs reached 7.5 million votes in the 1936 presidential election.

He was killed by a doctor whose career he had ruined. Long's bodyguard fired 61 bullets into the doctor who still managed to fire the one shot that killed Long.

NAME: Father Charles Coughlin, 1891-1979

At first, in 1933, Coughlin supported Roosevelt but within two years he was an opponent, setting up the National Union for Social Justice. This organisation promised work and fair wages for all. He also proposed to **nationalise** all banks and introduce a national minimum wage.

Coughlin criticised the New Deal for not doing enough and labelled Roosevelt as 'anti-God' because he was not really helping the needy. His main influence came from his weekly broadcasts which attracted over 40 million listeners, especially from urban and lower middle-class America. However, many more people listened to Roosevelt's 'fireside chats' (see pages 36-37).

Father Charles Coughlin

NAME: Dr Francis Townsend, 1867-1960

Townsend gained much support from old people who, in 1934, had benefited little from the New Deal. He set up an organisation called 'Old Age Revolving Pension Plan', also known as the Townsend clubs, which had attracted five million members by 1953.

He proposed to introduce a two per cent tax on business transactions and the money raised would be used to finance his scheme. The scheme was to give $200 a month to every citizen over 60 who had retired. The plan was to encourage more people to retire and thus create more jobs for the unemployed. The scheme collapsed in 1936 when Townsend's business partner was found guilty of stealing from the funds.

Dr Francis Townsend

Source A: Texas poster advertising Townsend's old age pensions plan, photo taken in 1935

Tasks

1. *Source A shows a poster advertising Townsend's scheme. Draw a similar poster advertising the scheme put forward by either Long or Coughlin.*

2. *What can you learn about the weaknesses of the New Deal from the schemes introduced by these three individuals?*

3. *Which of the three individuals do you think provided the most serious opposition to Roosevelt and the New Deal? Give at least one reason for your choice.*

Why did the Supreme Court oppose the New Deal?

Source A: A cartoon of 1936 showing Roosevelt lassoing a Supreme Court Judge

What message is the cartoonist trying to get across?

THE LINE OF LEAST RESISTANCE

In many respects the Supreme Court provided the most serious opposition to the New Deal and did much to handicap Roosevelt's measures.

The Supreme Court

The American **Constitution** set up the Supreme Court to keep a check on both Congress and the president. It consists of nine judges, appointed for life, whose task it is to make sure laws passed by Congress do not break the Constitution, or act **unconstitutionally**. When a judge dies or retires a new judge is nominated by the president.

Constitution

The rules under which a country is governed.

Unconstitutionally

Breaking the rules or constitution.

The Supreme Court's Republican nature

One reason that the Supreme Court opposed some of Roosevelt's measures was that it was dominated by Republican judges. This was because from 1861 to 1933 there were only sixteen years of Democrat presidents and few opportunities to nominate Democrat judges.

Out of the sixteen cases concerning the 'alphabet agencies' which were tried by the Supreme Court in 1935 and 1936, the judges declared that in eleven, Roosevelt had acted unconstitutionally. In reality, he was using central or federal powers which the Constitution had not given him. Two cases show the opposition he faced.

The 'Sick Chickens' case, 1935

This involved four brothers, the Schechters, who ran a poultry business. In 1933 they signed the National Recovery Act (NRA) rules of fair prices, wages and competition. In 1935, the NRA took them to court for selling a batch of diseased chickens unfit for human consumption. The Schechters appealed to the Supreme Court which declared the NRA illegal because its activities were unconstitutional. It gave the federal government powers it should not have to interfere in state affairs, in this case the state of New York. As a result, 750 of the NRA codes were immediately scrapped.

The US v Butler case, 1936

In this case the Supreme Court declared the Agricultural Adjustment Act illegal. The judges decided that giving help to farmers was a matter for each state government, not the federal government. As a result all help to farmers ceased.

Roosevelt's attempts at reform

After his massive victory in the 1936 presidential election, Roosevelt decided that public opinion was behind his New Deal. Therefore in February 1937, he threatened to retire those judges in the Supreme Court who were over 70, and replace them with younger ones who supported his policies.

These attempts failed for two reasons. First, many saw this as unconstitutional. They saw the president as trying to destroy the position of the Supreme Court by packing it with his own supporters. Secondly, Roosevelt failed to consult senior members of his own party and many Conservative Democrats opposed his reform.

Nevertheless, in March/April 1937 the Supreme Court reversed the 'Sick Chickens' decision and accepted his Social Security Act which brought in old-age pensions and unemployment insurance (see page 46). On the other hand, the whole episode had damaged Roosevelt's reputation and lost him the support of some members of his own party.

Tasks

1. *Was Roosevelt right to reform the Supreme Court?*

Make a copy of the following table and write in reasons in both columns.

Roosevelt right to reform Supreme Court	Roosevelt wrong to reform Supreme Court

Now look at the completed table. On balance do you think he was right?

2. *You are one of Roosevelt's leading advisers in 1936. What advice would you give him about the Supreme Court? Write your advice in the form of a memo. Here is how you could set it out. Remember to fill in the information at the start of your memo.*

Memo

To: From:

Date: Subject:

Dear Mr President,

   I ....

Examination practice

Source A: A broadcast from Huey Long, January 1935

All the people of America have been invited to a barbecue. God invited us all to come and eat and drink all he wanted. Then what happened? Millionaire businessmen stepped up and took enough for 120,000,000 people and left only enough for 5,000,000, for all the 125,000,000 to eat. And so many millions must go hungry and without those good things that God gave us – unless we call on them to put some of it back.

Question 1 – source utility

How useful is Source A as evidence of opposition to the New Deal?   (8 marks)

How to answer
- First look at what is useful about the content of Source A.

Example
Source A is useful because it shows us Long's views about the distribution of wealth in the USA. He believes that it has been unfairly distributed with a few rich businessmen getting the most, leaving millions poor and hungry.

Notice how the answer begins with 'Source A is useful'. This shows the examiner that the question is focused on utility.

- Then look at whether there are any limitations to the contents.

Example
Source A is of limited use because Long generalises about the distribution of wealth and gives a one-sided view of businessmen and the way they seized the wealth of the country. He makes no mention of businessmen who cared for the poor. The source makes no mention of Long's 'Share Our Wealth' movement.

Again, notice how the answer focuses immediately on the question. So far we have a good Level 2 answer.

Nature, origins and purpose (NOP)

In order to reach higher level marks for this question you have to explain the value (usefulness) and limitations of the NOP of each source. The nature and origins are found in the **provenance** of the source – the information given above or below it. These, in turn, should help you work out its purpose. A good tip is to highlight or underline key words in the provenance.

NOP means:

N   Nature of the source
What type of source is it? A speech, a photograph, a cartoon, a letter, an extract from a diary? How will the nature of the source affects its utility? For example, a private letter is often very useful because the person who wrote it generally gives their honest views.

O   Origins of the source
Who wrote or produced the source? Are their views worth knowing? Are they giving a one-sided view? When was it produced? It could be an eyewitness account. What are the advantages and disadvantages of eyewitness accounts?

P   Purpose of the source
For what reason was the source produced? For example, the purpose of adverts is to make you buy the products. People usually make speeches to get your support. How will this affect the utility of the source?

Now let us apply this to Source A.

• First look at how useful the source is in its NOP.

Example

Source A is useful because it is part of a radio broadcast by Huey Long, one of the leading opponents of the New Deal made in 1935 (origins) and gives us a valuable insight into his views. It highlights one very effective method, radio broadcasting (nature), which he used to criticise the New Deal and clearly shows how he tried to discredit the wealthy in order to win over the poor (purpose).

• Then look at whether the source has any limitations in its NOP.

Example

Source A is of limited use because it is an extract from a radio broadcast (nature) by an individual who was opposed to Roosevelt and the New Deal (origin), who was deliberately exaggerating (purpose) the distribution of wealth and distorting the position of businessmen in order to win support for his own 'Share Our Wealth' scheme.

Source B: A 1937 newspaper cartoonist's view of Roosevelt's attempts to reform the Supreme Court

Question 2 – source utility

How useful is Source B as evidence of Roosevelt's attempts to reform the Supreme Court? (8 marks)

Now have a go yourself

Make a copy of the table below and use it to plan your answer. Remember:

• Content only Level 2: up to 6 marks
• Content and NOP to reach Level 3: 7–8 marks.

	Usefulness	Limitations
Contents *What view does the source give?* *According to your knowledge of this topic, do you think this is a typical/popular view?* *Is the view one-sided?* *If it is, whose view is not given?*		
NOP Nature		
Origins		
Purpose		

Examination practice

In the examination (Paper 2) you will be asked to explain the utility of two sources.

Source A: A poem about Roosevelt and his family written during the New Deal

The King is in the White House
Handing out his money
The Queen is on the front page
Looking very funny
Their knave is up in Boston
Picking up the plums
While the nation alphabetically
Is feeding all the bums?

Source B: A 1938 cartoon about the New Deal

Question 1 – the utility of two sources

How useful are Sources A and B as evidence of opposition attitudes to the New Deal? (8 marks)

How to answer
- Explain the utility of each source in turn.
- Explain the value and limitations of the contents of each source.
- Explain the value and limitations of the NOP of each source.
- In your conclusion give a final judgement on the relative value of the two sources.

Here is a writing frame to help you:

Source A is useful because (contents) . . .

Moreover, Source A is also useful because of (NOP) . . .

Source A has limitations including . . .

Source B is useful because (contents) . . .

Furthermore, Source B is also useful because of (NOP) . . .

Source B has limitations including . . .

In conclusion, Sources A and B are useful because they . . .

5 The successes and failures of the New Deal

Source A From *New Deal Thought*, written in 1966 by an historian, H Zinn, who criticises the New Deal

When the reform energies of the New Deal began to wane around 1939 and the Depression was over, the nation was back to its normal state: a permanent army of unemployed and twenty or thirty million poverty-stricken people locked from public view by a prosperous middle class.

Source B From *America in the Twentieth Century*, written in 1989 by another historian, J Patterson

Roosevelt was concerned [about] more than improving his own position. He wanted to help ordinary people and he expressed their needs in simple language they could understand. In his 'fireside chats' and his numerous press conferences he put across the image of a man who cared. His air of confidence gave people hope and restored their faith in democracy. His New Deal measures did much to revive the economy and get the country out of its worst depression.

As you can see from Sources A and B, historians disagree about the New Deal.

- Some believe it was mainly a success and brought the USA out of the Depression.
- Others argue it only provided short-term solutions and that it was the Second World War which really re-generated the US economy.

You might be asked in the examination to judge the success of the New Deal. Did it achieve its aims of Reform, Relief and Recovery?

This chapter will consider the following questions:

- What impact did the New Deal have on the role of government and the president?
- Did it improve the economy of the USA?
- Was it successful in solving the problem of high unemployment?
- How important were the measures dealing with social welfare and industrial relations?
- Did it do anything to improve the position of women and black Americans?

Source skills

You will also be given guidance in answering the last and most difficult source question on the exam paper – the synthesis question in which you have to use the sources and your own knowledge to discuss an interpretation.

Key areas	Successes of the New Deal	Failures of the New Deal
Role of government and the president	• Restored the faith of people in government after the laissez-faire approach of Hoover. • Preserved democracy and ensured there was no mass support of right-wing politicians. • Greatly extended the role of central government and the president.	The New Deal divided the USA. Roosevelt: • gave too much power to the federal government and the presidency • ignored the position of the state governments • tried to change the membership and role of the Supreme Court • and his supporters were even accused of being communists.
Economy	• Stabilised the US banking system • Cut the number of business failures. • New Deal projects greatly improved the **infrastructure** of the USA by providing roads, schools and power stations.	• The New Deal only provided short-term solutions and did not solve the underlying economic problems. • Furthermore, the US economy took longer to recover than that of most European countries. When, in 1937, Roosevelt reduced the New Deal Budget, the country went back into depression.
Unemployment	The Alphabet Agencies (see page 36) provided work for millions with unemployment falling from a peak of 24.9 million in 1933, to 14.3 million four years later.	The Alphabet Agencies only provided short-term jobs. Once these ended, people were back on the dole. Even at its best in 1937, there were still over 14 million out of work and the number reached 19 million in the following year. It was the Second World War that brought an end to unemployment.
Industrial workers	The NRA (see page 39) and the Second New Deal (see page 45) greatly strengthened the position of labour unions and made corporations negotiate with them.	Unions were still treated with great suspicion by employers. Indeed, many strikes were broken up with brutal violence in the 1930s. Large corporations employed 'heavies' to deal with union leaders.
Social welfare	The Social Security Act (see page 46) provided the USA with a semi-welfare state which included pensions for the elderly and widows and state help for the sick and disabled.	Some argued that social welfare measures put too much pressure on taxpayers and destroyed self-esteem and the idea of 'rugged individualism'. It encouraged people to 'sponge' off the state.
Black Americans	Around 200,000 black Americans gained benefits from the CCC (see page 38) and other New Deal Agencies. Many benefited from slum clearance programmes and housing projects.	• Many New Deal agencies discriminated against black people. They either got no work, received worst treatment or lower wages. • Roosevelt did little to end **segregation** and discrimination in the deep South. For example, he failed to pass laws against the lynching of black Americans in case he alienated Democratic **senators** from the southern states. During nearly 15 years as president, Roosevelt only passed one law for black people.
Women	Some women achieved prominent positions in the New Deal: • Eleanor Roosevelt became an important campaigner for social reform. • Frances Perkins was the first woman to be appointed to a cabinet post as Secretary of Labour.	The New Deal offered little to women: • Some of the National Industry Recovery Act codes of 1933 actually required women to be paid less than men. • Only 8,000 women were employed by the CCC out of 2.75 million involved in the scheme. • Some state governments tried to avoid social security payments to women by introducing special qualifications.

Tasks

Read the table above.

1. *What opinion would the following have of the New Deal? Would they see it as a success, a failure or have mixed views? Draw a cartoon representing each with a speech bubble giving their views.*
   A trade union leader; the head of a large corporation; a member of a state government; a black worker; a single woman; an old couple.

2. *What would be your final judgement? Was the New Deal a success or a failure? You could use a concept map to organise your answer.*

Examination practice

The sources on this page and the following page will be used in the examination practice questions on pages 62–63.

Source A: From *The Assignment I'll Never Forget*, by photographer Dorothea Lange, who visited California in 1936. Here she is describing what she saw and photographed as she toured the USA

I approached the hungry woman ... She told me she was 32. She said she had been living on frozen vegetables from surrounding fields and birds that her children had killed. She had just sold the tyres from the car to buy food.

Source B: From a letter written to Roosevelt in 1935, explaining the benefits of the New Deal

Dear Mr President,
This is just to tell you everything is all right now. The man you sent found our house all right and we went down to the bank with him and the mortgage can go on for a while longer. You remember we wrote to you about losing the furniture too. Well, your man got it back for us. I never heard of a president like you Mr Roosevelt.

Source C: A cartoon about the achievements of the NRA, September 1933

Source D: Unemployment and the performance of the US economy, between 1929 and 1942

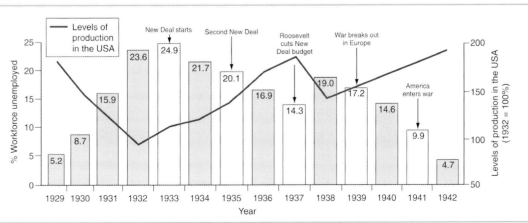

Source E: A photograph of black people queuing for government relief in front of a famous government poster, taken in 1937

WORLD'S HIGHEST STANDARD OF LIVING

There's no way like the American Way

Source F: From *Roosevelt and the New Deal*, D O'Callaghan, 1966

Before the Depression most had thought of government as a kind of policeman whose job was simply to keep order. Roosevelt, however, taught Americans to look to the governments they had elected to see that everyone had a fair chance to obtain what he called 'the good things of life'. He gave the American people renewed faith in their country's way of life.

Using Sources A to F on pages 61–62, answer these four different source questions, which are in the style of Paper 2 questions.

1. What can you learn from Source A about the effects of the New Deal? (4 marks)
2. Does Source C support the evidence of Sources A and D about the effects of the New Deal? Explain your answer. (6 marks)
3. How useful are Sources B and E as evidence of the effects of the New Deal? (8 marks)
4. 'The New Deal failed completely to solve the problems facing the USA in the years 1933 to 1941'. Use the sources, and your own knowledge, to explain whether you agree with this view. (12 marks)

Before attempting question 4, read the following advice on answering this type of question.

Question 4 – synthesis question

In question 4 you are asked to explain an interpretation using:

- the six sources
- your own knowledge.

This is worth the most marks (12) and the examiner would expect you to write a minimum of one side of A4.

- If you only use the sources *or* your own knowledge in your answer then the maximum you can be awarded is half (6) marks. Use both.
- You can achieve a good Level 3 mark (8–10) by agreeing *or* disagreeing as long as you use the sources *and* your own knowledge.
- To reach Level 4 (11–12 marks) you have to give both sides and use the sources *and* your own knowledge *and* judgement.

Planning your answer

Make a copy of the grid below and use it to help you plan your answer.

	Agrees with interpretation	Disagrees with interpretation
Sources		Source F because it shows how much Roosevelt did for the people.
Own knowledge	The New Deal did little for women.	

- First of all study once again all the sources on pages 61–62.
  - Which sources agree with the interpretation? Why? Give a brief explanation in the grid.
  - Which sources disagree with the interpretation? Why? Give a brief explanation in the grid. An example is given in the grid above.

- Now use your own knowledge of the New Deal and its successes and criticisms. To help you, look again at the table on page 60.
  - What knowledge can you use to agree with the interpretation? Summarise this in your grid. An example is given in the grid on page 62.
  - What knowledge can you use to disagree with the interpretation? Summarise this in your grid.
- To help prompt your own knowledge during an examination, underline any dates or facts in the sources which you could expand on in the answer. Expanding on sources will be classed as your own knowledge.

Writing your answer
Use the following guidelines.

Introduction
Explain the two possible sides to the interpretation.

> ## Example
> *There are various interpretations of the New Deal. Some believe it did little to solve the long-term problems brought by the Depression. Others, however, believe . . . (How could you finish the introduction?)*

Agreeing with the interpretation
- First use the sources.

> ## Example
> *Source E seems to agree with the interpretation because it shows a great number of black Americas queuing for relief in 1937.*

- Then use your own knowledge.

> ## Example
> *Black Americans gained little from the New Deal. Indeed some New Deal Agencies actually discriminated against black people who often got no work or received less wages than white people.*

- Try to add another paragraph of your own knowledge agreeing with the interpretation.

Disagreeing with the interpretation
Now use the sources and your own knowledge to disagree with the interpretation.

- Once again, use the sources first.

> ## Example
> *Source B does not agree with the interpretation as the writer emphasises the achievements of Roosevelt and his New Deal, especially how it restored people's faith in the government and gave them hope.*

- Expand on any facts/dates in the sources to bring in your own knowledge.

> ## Example
> *In addition, I disagree with the interpretation because the New Deal greatly improved the infrastructure of the USA including the building of roads, schools, bridges and power stations.*

- Try to add another paragraph of your own knowledge disagreeing with the interpretation.

Conclusion
Your final judgement on the interpretation. Do you mainly agree or disagree? Explain your judgement.

> ## Example
> *For the most part I disagree with the interpretation. I believe that the New Deal provided at least short-term relief for many US citizens and helped to kickstart the economy after the disastrous effects of the Depression. Roosevelt greatly expanded the role of the central government and showed people that he cared.*

The Divided Union? The USA, 1941–80

Three civil rights supporters sit at a lunch counter reserved for whites in Jackson, Mississippi, in May 1961. One white youth is about to pour a can of drink over the head of the woman in the middle. They have already been covered with sauce and mustard.

Tasks

1. *What can you learn about the USA in 1963 from this photo?*

2. *Does the photo show a 'divided union'?*

This section examines the key developments in the USA during the years 1941–80. It was a period in which there were many tensions in US society, including the campaign for civil rights and the student and women's protest movement. The real divisions, however, were exemplified by very contrasting attitudes to US involvement in the war in Vietnam. This is why it is often described as the 'Divided Union'. It also sees the emergence of powerful and charismatic figures such as Martin Luther King, Malcolm X and John F Kennedy. The outline study explains these developments and divisions in US society with each chapter posing key questions on one significant issue or change.

Chapter 6 The impact of the Second World War on the US economy and society (pages 67–76)

- Why did the US economy benefit so much from the war?
- Was there any progress in civil rights for women and black Americans?
- How were Japanese-Americans treated?

Chapter 7 McCarthyism and the 'red scare' (pages 77–86)

- What was meant by McCarthyism and why did it bring such widespread support?
- What methods did McCarthy use?
- Why did McCarthy lose support?

Chapter 8 Civil rights in the USA, 1941–80 (pages 87–106)

- What progress was made, especially in the 1950s, and what methods were used?
- What role did Martin Luther King play in the 1950s and 1960s?
- Why did the Black Power movement emerge in the 1960s? What part was played by Malcolm X?
- What progress was made in the 1960s?
- Why was there serious urban unrest in the mid and later 1960s?

Chapter 9 The 'New Frontier' and the 'Great Society' (pages 107–118)

- What was meant by John F Kennedy's 'New Frontier'?
- What did it achieve? Why was his death such a shock to US society?
- What was meant by Lyndon Johnson's 'Great Society'?
- What did he achieve and why did he arouse so much opposition?

Chapter 10 Protest movements in the 1960s and 1970s (pages 119–132)

- Why did these protest movements emerge?
- What were the key features and achievements of these movements?
- What links were there between the different movements?

Chapter 11 The Watergate scandal and its impact (pages 133–141)

- Why did the scandal take place?
- What were the key developments?
- What effects did the scandal have on US society, especially attitudes to politics?

Outline study questions

There are a number of different types of questions to answer on Paper 1, four in Section (a) and two in Section (b). Here are examples from the June 2004 Paper. Each set of questions is divided into two sections:

Section (a) – short mini-essay type questions (this page).

Section (b) – two essay questions (page 66).

PAPER 1

EXAM
The USA Outline Study

A photograph of the 'Hollywood Ten' and their two lawyers.

Look at the photograph and then answer all the questions which follow.

(a) (i) What was meant by the term 'Hollywood Ten'?

(3 marks)

(ii) Why were the cases of Alger Hiss and the Rosenbergs important in the growing fear of communism within the USA?

(5 marks)

(iii) Describe the key features of the methods used by Senator McCarthy to win the support of US citizens in the early 1950s.

(5 marks)

(iv) Why had Senator McCarthy lost the support of the US Senate and most US citizens by the end of 1954?

(7 marks)

(Total 20 marks)

...efinition ...estion (you ...ve to explain ...e meaning of a ...rd or term). ...nother ...troductory ...estion worth ...ree marks is ...e **reason** ...estion, where ...u must 'give ...e reason'.

...y features ...estion (this ...eans the most ...portant events ...developments).

A **causation** question (you have to give reasons). Another type of five- or seven-mark question asks 'In what ways . . . ?' (you have to make points).

This is another **causation** question. It is worth seven marks which means explaining more reasons than in the five-mark question.

This is known as the scaffolding question. The examiner has given you a scaffold (four factors) to write about.

EXAM

PAPER 1 — The USA Outline Study

(b) Part (b) of this question is about the USA in the years 1945–68.

(i) In what ways did US citizens secure improved civil rights in the years 1945–63?

You may use the following information to help you with your answer:

Impact of Second World War

1954 Brown v Topeka

1957 Events at Little Rock High School

The work of Martin Luther King

(15 marks)

(ii) Choose two items from the boxes below and explain why they were important in the USA in the 1960s.

The 'New Frontier'	1964: Civil Rights Act	1965: Voting Rights Act

(10 marks)

(Total 25 marks)

This is a **ten-mark essay** question in which you have to make a judgement on the importance of two factors.

Essay writing/planning skills

As you can see, Paper 1 tests not only your knowledge and understanding but also your essay-writing skills. Each question is asking you to organise your knowledge to ensure you focus your answer to a particular question. For example, the last question is not asking you to write everything you know about two of these factors. Instead you have to explain the importance of each.

It is therefore important that you get into the habit of:

- planning your answers, especially to the essays in Section (b), before you write
- developing your essay-writing skills.

You will be given advice on all of these questions during the course of Chapters 6–11.

6 The impact of the Second World War on the US economy and society

Part of Pearl Harbor after the Japanese attack, 7 December 1941.

After the First World War, the USA pursued a policy of isolationism. It did not want to be involved in European disputes that would drag it into another war. This continued after the outbreak of the Second World War in Europe in September 1939. Then, on 7 December 1941, the Japanese launched an attack on the American fleet at Pearl Harbor, Hawaii, resulting in the death of 2,400 Americans and the loss of eight battleships. Within four days, the USA was at war with Japan, Germany and Italy.

The war brought about important economic and social changes.

By the end of this chapter you will be able to answer the following questions:

- Why and how did the US economy benefit so much from the war?
- Why were Japanese-Americans often treated so badly?
- What effects did the war years have on the position of women in American society?
- Did black Americans make any progress in their position in American society during the war years?

Exam skills

You will practice answering the first type of question on Paper 1 (a **definition** question), worth three marks, which can ask you to either:

- explain/define a term
- explain one reason or consequence.

How did the war benefit the US economy?

Changes in the role of government

The New Deal had greatly increased the role of the federal government in the economy (see Chapter 2) and this was further extended during the war. For example, in 1942, Roosevelt, who was president from 1933 to 1945, set up the War Production Board under the **industrialist** William Knudsen, to organise and provide for the needs of war, more especially the needs of the armed forces. To help promote support for the war, the government set up schemes such as the Office for Civilian Defence, which asked the American people to 'give an hour a day for the USA'. By 1945, the government employed almost four million civilian workers, almost double the number in 1941. The majority of Americans were prepared to accept this increased role even when the war ended.

Big business and the war effort

Roosevelt was determined to make use of leading US businessmen to provide for the needs of war. The War Production Board was run by William Knusden, a leading industrialist. Henry J Kaiser, another important industrialist, had been heavily involved in the Tennessee Valley Authority which was set up in the mid 1930s to develop the Tennessee Valley. It organised the building of 33 dams to control the Tennessee River (see pages 41–42) and was made responsible for the USA's metal and shipbuilding industries.

Roosevelt called in other industrialists to ask their advice on meeting the needs of war production and setting targets, allowing them to decide which companies would produce particular goods. For example, **General Motors** produced heavy machine guns and thousands of other war products. Indeed, the vast majority of contracts went to larger firms. In return, the firms made a lot of money.

Source A: From the diary of Henry Stimson, the US Secretary of War, 1941

*If we are going to go to war in a **capitalist country** you've got to let business make money out of the process or business won't work.*

Bond

A certificate of debt issued in order to raise funds. It carries a fixed rate of interest.

Capitalist country

A country in which businesses are owned privately and people are able to make a profit.

Depression

A period of extended and severe decline in a nation's economy, marked by low production and high unemployment.

General Motors

One of the largest car manufacturers in the USA.

Industrialist

Someone who owns and/or runs an industry or factory.

Munitions

Ammuntion/weapons produced for the armed forces.

The New Deal

The name given to the policies introduced by President Roosevelt in the 1930s to solve the problems created by the Depression.

The impact of the war on the US economy

Wartime production

The USA became the arsenal of the Allied powers. Roosevelt believed that to win a modern war you had to have more of everything than your opponents. Traditional industries such as coal, iron, steel and oil greatly expanded due to government contracts. In 1939, the USA had a very small air-force of just 300 planes. In 1944, the USA built 96,000 aircraft in one year alone, more than Germany and Japan together. Between 1941 and 1945, American factories produced:

- 250,000 aircraft
- 90,000 tanks
- 350 naval destroyers
- 200 submarines
- 5,600 merchant ships.

Indeed, by 1944 the USA was producing almost half the weapons in the world.

Source B: B-24 bombers on the assembly line in Detroit, Michigan, November 1943

The impact on the workforce and unemployment

Around sixteen million American men and women served in the US armed forces, so many more workers were needed on the home front. This, in turn, put an end to the serious unemployment caused by the **Depression**. In 1939, unemployment stood at 9.5 million. By 1944, it had fallen to just 670,000. Fourteen million worked in the factories. For example, General Motors took on an extra 750,000 workers during the war. Nearly four million workers, many of these black Americans, **migrated** from the rural South to the industrial North.

Probably the greatest change was in the employment of women. Although there were already 12 million working women, a further seven million joined the workforce, taking on jobs from which they had previously been excluded. For example, one in three aircraft workers were women, and half of those working in electronics and **munitions** were also women.

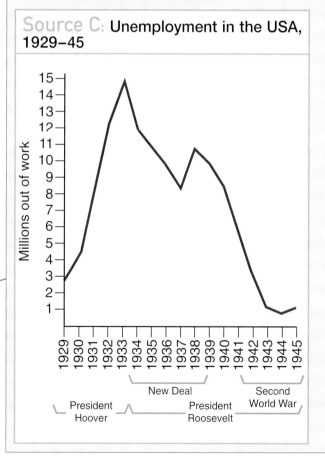

Source C: Unemployment in the USA, 1929–45

General benefits

Of all the countries involved in fighting the Second World War, the USA was the only one that became stronger economically. More than half a million new businesses were set up. American farmers enjoyed much better times as the US exported food to help its Allies. The US government raised the money to finance the war by raising taxes but also by selling **bonds** to the public (see Source D). Those buying the bonds were guaranteed their money back after a set period plus a guaranteed rate of interest. By the end of the war, Americans had bought bonds totalling $129 billion.

There was a downside as US citizens had to accept rationing. Rationing, however, did not have as huge an impact as in Europe and Japan.

Source D: **A US government poster advertising war bonds, December 1941**

Tasks

1. *Study Source D. What can you learn from it about government bonds? (Remember your inference skills, see page 20.)*

2. *Look at Sources A to D (pages 68–70). Which source is the most useful as evidence of the impact of the Second World War on the US economy? Explain your choice.*

3. *Prepare a one-minute talk summarising the main effects of the Second World War on the US economy.*

- *What are the key developments to include?*
- *You may use bullet points or prefer to write out a script.*
- *Practice the timing of the talk. It must last no longer than one minute.*

Examination practice

Question 1 – reason

Give one reason to explain why the economy benefited from US involvement in the Second World War.   (3 marks)

This is an example of an introductory question you will have to answer on Paper 1. It is worth three marks.

How to answer
- Focus on the key issue in the question.

For this question it is *one reason for the growth of the US economy.*

- Begin your answer by giving the reason.

Example
One reason why the US economy benefited from the Second World War was because of increased production.

- Now give an explanation for this reason. Be as precise as you can in order to achieve the maximum three marks.

Example
By 1944, the US economy was producing almost half of the weapons made in the world. Between 1941 and 1945, American factories produced 250,000 aircraft, 90,000 tanks and 350 naval destroyers. Traditional industries such as coal, iron, steel, oil and shipbuilding greatly expanded due to the government contracts for war materials.

Question 2

Now have a go yourself

Give one reason why the role of the federal government changed during the Second World War.   (3 marks)

How were Japanese-Americans treated?

The USA had a large Japanese immigrant population, mainly on the Pacific coast. However, the Japanese attack on Pearl Harbor brought a wave of anti-Japanese feeling from most, but not all, Americans. Some, on the West Coast, who knew the Japanese immigrants well, were more sympathetic. Yet the majority believed anti-Japanese propaganda, which was used to drum up support for the war and encourage volunteers for the armed forces, and saw many Japanese residents as potential spies and, at the very least, a threat to internal security.

Source A: A poster from Texaco, 1942, which was posted in factories

What image is given of the Japanese?

TOKIO KID
SAY

MIXED RIVETS MAKE S[...] HAPPY[...] THANK YOU

Conscripted
Where males of a certain age (usually 18–41) have to serve in the armed forces for a period of time.

Internment camps
Effectively prison camps.

Reactions to these measures

The policy came under criticism at the time. For example, in 1944, a US Supreme Court judge called it 'government racism'.

- It did not differentiate between Issei – foreign-born Japanese (about one-third of the Japanese-American population) – and Nisei, that is children of Issei, born in the USA.
- In some US states, Japanese people faced vandalism and even murder.
- Chinese-Americans were often subjected to attacks because people thought they looked Japanese.
- The USA was at war with Italy and Germany – no Germans or Italians were interned.

In 1988, the US **Congress** agreed on an apology for the policy and gave $20,000 compensation each to all surviving internees.

US government measures

In the spring of 1942, more than 100,000 Japanese-Americans were moved from their homes to relocation camps in bleak parts of the USA. Many of them lost their property, or were forced to sell at very low prices. They were then moved to **internment camps**.

In the internment camps the Japanese-Americans acted with great dignity and patriotism. They raised the Stars and Stripes flag each morning. At the same time, more than 8,000 Japanese-Americans were **conscripted** and 9,000 volunteered to fight for the USA. In addition the 442nd Regimental Combat Team, almost entirely made up of Japanese-Americans, was the most decorated combat force in the US army.

Tasks

1. *Give one reason to explain why Japanese-Americans were interned in 1942.*

(Remember how to answer this question? See page 70.)

2. *You are an editor of a West Coast newspaper in 1942, who sympathises with Japanese-Americans. Put together the front page of your newspaper with a headline and leading article that encourages opposition to the policy of internment.*

Did the war benefit women?

Before 1941, American women had a traditional role as wives and mothers, with few women following careers. There were few real career opportunities except in typically 'female' professions such as teaching, nursing and secretarial work.

Socially, however, the 1920s had seen much progress especially in urban areas. Some women wore more daring clothes, smoked and drank with men in public. They went out with men, in cars, without a chaperone and even kissed in public. In addition, in 1921 women over 20 were given the vote.

How did women help with the war effort?

Women made a great contribution to the war effort and this opened up many new areas of employment for working class women, especially in producing munitions. Indeed, the pay in 'munitions' work was much higher than that normally paid to women in 'female' occupations. The number of women employed increased from 12 million in 1940 to 18.5 million, five years later. Many of these new jobs were in traditionally 'male' occupations such as the shipyards, aircraft factories and munitions. Women proved that they could do these jobs and, in 1942, a poll showed that 60 per cent of Americans were in favour of women helping with the war industries.

Women also joined the armed forces, with about 300,000 serving in the women's sections of the army, navy and the nursing corps.

Did the position of women improve?

In certain respects it did. Women had shown they could do jobs which traditionally had been male dominated. Four US states made equal pay for women compulsory, while other states tried to protect women from discrimination in their jobs. In 1940, women made up 19 per cent of the workforce. This had risen to 28.8 per cent ten years later.

Nevertheless, at the end of the war:

- The majority of women willingly gave up their wartime jobs and returned to their role as mothers and wives and their traditional 'female' jobs.
- Women were generally excluded from the top, well-paid jobs.
- Women, on average, earned 50–60 per cent of the wage that men earned for doing the same job.
- Women could still be dismissed from their job when they married.

Source A: A poster from wartime USA featuring Rosie the Riveter, 1942

'Rosie the Riveter' was a fictional female worker used by the US government in a poster campaign to encourage women to help with the war effort. Hollywood even made a movie about Rosie.

We Can Do It!

WAR PRODUCTION CO-ORDINATING COMMITTEE

Source B: Peggy Terry describing her work in a munitions factory in Kentucky during the Second World War

I pulled a lot of gadgets on a machine. Tetryl was one of the ingredients we used and it turned us orange. Our hands, our face, our neck just turned orange, even our eyeballs. We never questioned … The only thing we worried about was other women thinking we had dyed our hair. Back then it was a disgrace if you dyed your hair. I remember a woman on a bus saying that she hoped the war would not end until she got her refrigerator paid for.

Source C: US service women, 1944, who were in a contest to find the most attractive woman in the US armed forces

Tasks

Study Sources A, B and C.

1. *What can you learn from Source C about the role of women during the war? (Use your inference skills, see page 20.)*

2. *Copy and fill in the following table by studying sources A, B and C. For each source decide whether it shows progress in the position of women or a lack of progress. Give a brief explanation for your choice. You may feel that one or more of the sources show both.*

3. *Give one reason why the position of women changed during the Second World War.*

(Do you remember how to do this type of question? If not, look again at the examination practice box on page 70.)

Source	Progress	Lack of progress

Did the war benefit black Americans?

The war provided black Americans with a good opportunity to push for **civil rights**. But how much progress, if any, did they make in ending **discrimination** and **segregation** and achieving civil rights?

The Double V campaign

The **Congress of Racial Equality** (CORE) was set up in 1942 to use non-violent protest to achieve black civil rights. It started to organise sit-ins against segregated restaurants and theatres. The black press set up the 'Double V' campaign. This would involve victory at home in terms of civil rights as well as abroad on the battlefield.

One leading campaigner was Philip Randolph. He led blacks in their struggle for equality using the slogan 'We loyal American citizens demand the right to work and fight for our country'. He set up the 'March on Washington Movement' and hoped to attract up to 100,000 people. This was to be a mass march on Washington together with a possible strike to try to make the government bring an end to discrimination in the workplace.

The Fair Employment Practice Committee (FEPC)

The government was alarmed at the possibility of a mass strike and came up with a compromise. Randolph called off the march. In return, Roosevelt agreed to ban discrimination against blacks in industrial and government jobs and set up a Fair Employment Practice Committee to report on discrimination. The FEPC discovered widespread discrimination within a number of companies and, although it could not force such companies to employ black people, it could use the threat of withdrawing government contracts.

The armed forces

The war highlighted the racism and discrimination in the armed forces, especially as the USA was fighting against a racist state, Nazi Germany. Black soldiers stationed in Britain were treated far better than back home. In the army, there were black-only units with white officers.

Before 1944, black soldiers were not allowed into combat in the marines. They were employed to transport supplies, or as cooks and labourers. Many black women served in the armed forces as nurses but were only allowed to treat black soldiers. The US Air Force would not accept black pilots.

Discrimination was worst in the navy, with black soldiers given the most dangerous job of loading ammunition on ships bound for war zones. For example, in 1944 a horrific accident killed 323 people – most of them black sailors. Few became officers.

Source A: Black American soldiers in action in 1944, during the Second World War

However, there was progress as the US Supreme Commander, General Eisenhower, supported **integrated combat units**:

- From 1944, black soldiers were fighting in integrated combat units and there were hundreds of black officers in the army and marines.
- By 1945, there were many integrated combat units.
- There were also fighter squadrons of black pilots, although they were not allowed to fly in the same groups as whites.
- By the end of the war, 58 black sailors had risen to the rank of officer.

Source B: This 'prayer' appeared in a black newspaper in January 1943

Draftee's prayer

Dear Lord, today
I go to war:
To fight, to die
Tell me what for
Dear Lord, I'll fight,
I do not fear
Germans or Japs,
My fears are here.
America.

Continued discrimination

Over 400,000 black Americans migrated from the South to the USA's industrial centres, where they continued to face discrimination and prejudice. Black workers generally only earned half of what white workers earned. This led to racial tension with **race riots** in 47 cities, the worst of which was in Detroit in 1943. On 21 June, 25 black and nine white people were killed. More than 700 people were injured and there was $2 million worth of damage to property. In the same year, nine black Americans were killed in riots in Harlem, New York.

There were also riots at nine black army-training camps, where the soldiers resented their unequal treatment.

The situation at the end of the war

There had been some progress in employment and the armed forces, and many blacks had become more active in campaigning for civil rights. On the other hand, discrimination and segregation remained a way of life in the southern states, whilst the migration of many black Americans to the industrial cities of the North had created greater racial tension.

Source C: Notice in Detroit during the riots of June 1943

Tasks

1. Look at the sources on page 75. Does Source C support the evidence of Sources A and B about the progress made by black Americans during the Second World War? Explain your answer. (Remember your cross-referencing skills – see page 27.)

2. Give one reason why black Americans made progress during the Second World War.

(Do you remember how to do this type of question? If not, look again at page 70.)

3. Copy the table below. From the information in this chapter fill in the table with key words to indicate benefits and lack of progress. Some examples have been done for you. There may be more than one benefit or lack of progress for each different group. In the last column, using a scale of 1–5 make a judgement on how much progress was made, with a brief comment, with 5 = great benefit, and 1 = no benefit.

	Benefits	Lack of progress	Extent of progress
Federal government			
Industrialists	Given war contracts		5 Many made huge profits
Workers			
Black Americans		Still discrimination in workplace	
Women			
Japanese-Americans			

Examination practice

Question 1 – definition
What was meant by the 'Double V' campaign during the Second World War?   (3 marks)

How to answer
This is an example of the other type of introductory question in Paper 1 in which you are asked to explain the meaning of a term.

• Give a precise definition of the term.

Example
The 'Double V' campaign meant campaign for victory in two ways, victory abroad in the war and victory at home in the campaign for civil rights.

• Explain it by putting it in the context of the time.

Example
One of its leading campaigners was Philip Randolph who tried to organise a mass march to Washington and a strike to pressurise the government into ending discrimination in the workplace.

Question 2 – definition
What was meant by the Fair Employment Practice Committee?   (3 marks)

What is wrong with the following answer?

Answer
The Fair Employment Practice Committee was set up to stop discrimination.

Now you have a go at the question.

7 McCarthyism and the 'red scare'

Source A A cartoon of 1947 showing a person taking a loyalty oath

YEAH — SO HELP ME GOD!

LOYALTY OATH

Task

Look at Source A.

What can you learn from Source A about attitudes to those who were taking loyalty oaths?

The Bolshevik Revolution of October 1917 in Russia caused many Americans to fear a similar event in their own country. This fear did not go away, even when the two countries were Allies united against Adolf Hitler. After the Second World War, the fear of the growth of communism in the USA became ever stronger. The advance of the Soviet armies and their reluctance to withdraw from Eastern Europe indicated to President Truman that he would have to be firm in his dealings with Stalin. The Truman Doctrine, Marshall Plan, Berlin Airlift, Hollywood Ten and the Alger Hiss case were clear examples that the Soviet Union and the spread of communism had to be thwarted at all costs.

This chapter will answer the following questions:

- Why was there a fear of communism in the USA, and in what ways did events outside the USA and the cases of Hiss and the Rosenbergs within it, contribute to this fear?
- Why was McCarthy able to win so much support, so easily?
- Why did McCarthyism fade away?
- What were the effects of McCarthyism?

Exam skills

You will practise Paper 1 **causation** questions worth seven marks.
There will be some 'Why...?' questions and a focus on what the examiner is looking for, as well as the descriptive type of questions – 'In what ways...?'.

Why was there a fear of communism?

Source A: A cartoon published in the USA in 1919 entitled 'Come on!'

The American Legion was a patriotic organisation formed in 1919. What can you learn about US attitudes to the threat of revolution at this time?

Attorney General
Chief legal officer of the US government.

Bolsheviks
The political group led by Lenin. They believed in communism.

Communism
Political theory which put forward the idea of state ownership of industry and agriculture.

USSR/Soviet Union
Name given to Russia after the Bolshevik Revolution.

Key Terms

Shortly after the **Bolshevik** Revolution of 1917, a wave of violent anti-**communism** spread across the USA. The communist views held by Lenin and the Bolsheviks were despised by many US citizens. The ideas were completely against capitalism – the system on which the USA had flourished in the nineteenth and early twentieth centuries. Any attempt to spread Bolshevism into the USA was resisted wholeheartedly.

Bolshevik Revolution, 1917
In October 1917, the Bolshevik Party seized power and overthrew the Provisional Government. After a civil war which lasted almost four years, opponents were defeated and the Bolsheviks, led by Lenin, began to set up a communist state.

The 'red scare' of 1919 and 1920 in the USA (see page 83) was whipped up not only by the press, but also by public officials. President Wilson's **Attorney General**, A Mitchell Palmer, tried to clear out what he thought were communists – some Russian immigrants were sent back to their country of origin, thousands were arrested and, by the summer of 1920, it was felt that the spread of Bolshevism had been halted.

The hatred and fear of communism did not disappear completely. The United States did not recognise the government of the Union of Soviet Socialist Republics (**USSR**) until 1933. There was still a concern in the USA that the USSR wanted to destroy capitalism, and this seemed to be borne out when the **Soviet Union** invaded Poland in 1939 and went to war against Finland later that year.

The Second World War
However, the USA and USSR were thrown together as allies in 1941, after the USA entered the war following the Japanese attack on Pearl Harbor – yet the alliance remained uneasy and cautious. Stalin distrusted Roosevelt and the USA because there seemed to be an unwillingness to open the second front in Europe against Hitler.

At the Yalta conference in February 1945, the USA and USSR were able to make some agreements about their approach to the post-war world. However, Roosevelt and Stalin could not agree fully on the fate of Germany, nor could Roosevelt persuade Stalin to remove Soviet troops from Eastern Europe. Between Yalta and Roosevelt's death in April 1945, communist governments were set up in Soviet-held territories. Stalin thus broke his promises made at Yalta that he would allow free elections in Eastern Europe.

Harry Truman, the new president, did not think that the USSR could be trusted and his advisers urged him 'to get tough' with Stalin. At the Potsdam Conference in July 1945, Truman knew that the atomic bomb had been successfully tested and, in the words of Churchill, 'he generally bossed the whole meeting'. Truman did not feel that the alliance with the Soviet Union was now so important.

The aftermath of the war

The war ended in August 1945 and throughout the first months of peace, relations between the two Superpowers worsened and Truman was advised to 'contain Russian expansive tendencies'. In March 1946, Churchill talked of an 'iron curtain' separating the West and East in Europe – there seemed to be clear hostility between the former allies.

Events in Europe continued to widen the gap – the British inability to stem communism in Greece led President Truman to issue the Truman Doctrine, and the supreme effort to contain communism came with the Marshall Plan.

Truman Doctrine, 1947

President Truman's belief that communism was a worldwide threat, and the USA should meet it by helping all people whose freedom was threatened by communism.

Marshall Plan, 1947

General Marshall of the USA suggested that the USA should help European countries to rebuild their economies and more than $14 billion was given. The plan was the economic arm of the Truman Doctrine and the USA thought it would prevent the spread of communism.

Task

1. *What can you learn from Sources A and B about US attitudes to communism and the Soviet Union? (Remember your inference skills, see page 20.)*

Source B: An American pamphlet, depicting Stalin and the Soviet Union as an octopus stretching its tentacles around the globe

The Cold War begins

In 1948, the Soviet Union prevented the development of democracy in Czechoslovakia and ensured the Czech Communist Party was able to take control of the government. The Berlin Blockade of 1948–49 indicated that Stalin was prepared to risk war in the hope of removing the Allies from Berlin, when he stopped all land transport into the city. These events, and the Soviet development of the atom bomb, convinced the Americans that Stalin wanted world domination. Moreover, the success of the Communist Party in China in 1949, indicated the 'danger' of communism as a truly worldwide threat. As far as Truman and his advisers were concerned, the spread of communism had to be halted. The Western countries formed the North Atlantic Treaty Organisation (NATO), which stated that an attack on any NATO member was seen as an attack on the whole alliance. The 'cold war' was now being waged between the two **Superpowers**.

World events had woken up many Americans to the threat of communism and some of these people now saw a threat within the USA.

'The enemy within'

President Truman disliked communism and he often talked about 'the enemy within' – meaning inside the USA. His reaction in March 1947, to some Congressmen's accusations that he was soft on communists in the USA, was to introduce the Federal Employee Loyalty Programme (FELP). FELP was designed to check the security risks of people working in government. The checks did not uncover any cases of spying and, by 1952, more than 6.6 million federal workers had been examined. Around 3,000 were forced to resign and more than 200 were sacked.

Later in 1947, the House Un-American Activities Committee (HUAC) began to look into communist infiltration in the film industry. There was a fear that films were being used to put over a communist message. Ten writers and directors had to testify before HUAC and they were asked if they had ever been members of the Communist Party. They refused to answer, pleading the **Fifth Amendment** – the result was jail, because they were found to be in contempt of Congress. The 'Hollywood Ten' were sacked and spent a year in prison (see Source C, and look back at the photo on page 65).

(see Source C, and look back at the photo on page 65).

Fifth Amendment

Part of the US **constitution** which allows the accused person in a trial not to be forced to give testimony.

Superpowers

At the end of the war, the USA and USSR were so powerful in military and economic terms that they had left all other countries behind.

> **Source C: Written in prison in 1950 by Dalton Trumbo, one of the Hollywood Ten**
>
> *Say then but this of me:*
> *Preferring not to crawl on his knees*
> *In freedom to a bowl of buttered slops*
> *Set out for him by some contemptuous clown,*
> *He walked to jail on his feet.*
>
> *What does Trumbo mean in this short verse?*

What was the importance of the Hiss and Rosenberg cases?

Alger Hiss

Whittaker Chambers, an editor on *Time* magazine and a former communist, informed a leading member of HUAC, Richard Nixon, that Alger Hiss was a spy. Hiss had worked for a Supreme Court judge, was at Yalta with Roosevelt and in 1948 was working for a peace organisation. Hiss was interrogated and discredited by Nixon, but there was little evidence to prove him to be a spy.

Later that year, Nixon and one of his assistants were invited to Chambers' farm. Chambers had previously insisted that there had never been any espionage between himself and Hiss. However, at the farm, Chambers suddenly took Nixon and his aide to a pumpkin patch and pulled off the top of a pumpkin and took out a roll of microfilm. The microfilm had government documents, some of which had been copied on Hiss' typewriter. The documents became known as the 'Pumpkin Papers'. In 1950, Hiss was tried for perjury and sentenced to five years in jail and Nixon became known as a relentless pursuer of communists.

The Rosenbergs

The fear of communism continued to grow because the Soviet Union had exploded its first atom bomb in 1949. That same month, Julius Rosenberg was arrested on suspicion of spying and later tried on the charge of conspiring to commit espionage. His wife, Ethel, was arrested in August of that year on the same charges. The couple had been former members of the Communist Party but had no links by 1950. The government claimed that they were intending to give atomic secrets to the Soviet Union. Both were found guilty and sentenced to death. They spent two years on 'death row' and their appeals failed. They were executed on the same day in June 1953.

In September 1950, at the height of the Hiss case, the beginning of the Rosenberg issue and the worry over Korea, Congress passed the McCarran Internal Security Act.

The McCarran Internal Securty Act, 1950

- Communist Party had to register with the justice department to ensure that the party and its members could be carefully monitored.
- In the event of war, suspected communists could be held in detention camps.
- A Subversive Activities Control Board was set up to watch communist activities in the USA.
- Communists were not allowed to work in armament factories.

Examination practice

Question 1 – causation or 'why?'

Explain why a hatred of communism had developed in the USA by 1949.   (5 marks)

How to answer

- This is a 'Why?' question. Begin by using the question itself.

> **Example**
>
> *A hatred of communism had developed because …*

- In your answer you must use words which will signal to the examiner that you are presenting a clear/sharp and direct response. Try to include such words as 'because', 'reason', 'factor'. These will show the examiner that you are really answering the question.
- Plan your answer carefully – pick out the main points, list them and then place them in the correct time sequence. Remember to focus on 'why?'.
- When you finish your work, look at the answer and underline key words such as 'reason', 'because', 'factor' – then you know that you have answered the question.

Tasks

2. Write a poem protesting about the role of the government and the HUAC at the end of the Second World War.

3. What message did the McCarran Act send out to the people of the USA?

4. Conduct further research of your own and then put forward a case that both Hiss and the Rosenbergs were framed.

5. Construct a timeline from 1945–54, as shown below, which shows the key events in the fear of communism in the USA. Place events outside the USA on the top line and internal events ('the enemy within') below the line. Some events have been given as examples.

US drop atom bomb on Japan

1945	1946	1947	1948	1949	1950	1951	1952	1953	1954

McCarran Act

Why was McCarthy able to win support?

McCarthy showing the amount of communist activity in the USA in 1954. Why was such a photograph able to cause fear across the USA?

At the height of the fears in 1950, there appeared a **senator** who in a very short time created hysteria about communism. This was Senator Joseph McCarthy of Wisconsin.

On 9 February 1950, McCarthy addressed a **Republican** meeting in West Virginia and stated that he had the names of 205 communists who were working in the State Department, which dealt with foreign affairs. He also cited Owen Lattimore, a professor at one of the top US universities, as the 'top Russian spy'.

Over the following weeks his claims fluctuated, leading some people to question whether the claims could be supported. No names were produced apart from Lattimore's, and even he was cleared of any wrong-doing in 1955.

A **Senate** committee was set up to investigate the accusations and after several weeks, it decided that McCarthy's claims were 'a fraud and a hoax'. The committee chairman, Senator Tydings, was branded a communist by McCarthy and in the autumn, he was defeated in the senate elections by a supporter of McCarthy. From this point, many politicians were frightened to speak out against McCarthy.

Key Terms

Senate
The upper house of the US Congress.

Senator
Member of the Senate. There are two senators per state in the USA.

It was in this atmosphere that the McCarran Act (see page 81) was passed, despite President Truman's attempts to **veto** it (see Source A).

Source A: From President Truman's speech rejecting the McCarran Bill, 1950

There is no more basic truth in American life than the statement – 'In a free country we punish men for their crimes they commit but not for the opinions they have.'

The growth of McCarthy's influence

McCarthy was made Chairman of the Government Committee on Operations of the Senate and this allowed him to investigate state bodies and also interview hundreds of individuals about their political beliefs. His aim was to root out communists from the government, and his hearings and public statements destroyed the lives of many people.

Little evidence was produced – it was enough to be accused by him. Nevertheless, he won massive support across the USA and it is clear that in late 1952, his activities contributed to the Republicans' presidential victory.

Nixon

Nixon, as vice-presidential candidate, was quick to build on the hysteria created by McCarthy (see Source B). For Nixon, the issue would be a vote-winner not only for the Republicans but also for himself.

From a speech by Richard Nixon, Republican vice-president candidate, September 1952, indicating his intentions about the communist threat

What I intend to do is go up and down this land ... and expose the communists and crooks and those that defend them until they are all thrown out of Washington.

The 'red scare'

Some Congressmen jumped on the McCarthy bandwagon, and the HUAC still continued to seek out those who would undermine the USA. The attack on Hollywood continued, and many actors and writers were blacklisted and were unable to secure work for several years and in some cases ever again. It is estimated that there were about 50 films made between 1947 and 1954 which openly showed that communists were the enemy of the USA.

Various names have been given to this part of US history – the 'red scare', a time when there were 'reds under the bed', the 'witch hunt' and the 'international communist conspiracy'. The word 'red' was used because it had been used in the Russian Revolution and the Bolshevik forces had been known as the 'Red Army'. But the man who was the nation's most ardent anti-communist and had become the symbol of the 'red-hating crusader' gave his name to the era – McCarthyism.

McCarthy continued his work of hunting out communists and, in late 1952, his researchers investigated libraries to see whether they contained any anti-American books which might have been written by communists. As a result of the searches, many of these books were taken out of circulation.

Source C: **Harry S Truman speaking on the radio, 17 November 1953, about his views on McCarthyism**

McCarthyism ... the meaning of the word is the corruption of the truth, the abandonment of our historical devotion to fair play. It is the abandonment of 'due process' of law. It is the use of the big lie and the unfounded accusation against any citizen in the name of Americanism and security ... This horrible cancer is eating at the vitals of America and it can destroy the great edifice of freedom.

Source D: **Philip Reed, Head of General Electric, writing to President Eisenhower on 8 June 1953, describing how some European countries were concerned about the impact of McCarthyism inside the USA**

Reed was head of one of the most powerful companies in the USA and after a visit to Europe, he was concerned that the USA might find itself losing European customers. The memory of the Second World War was still very strong and at the height of the Cold War, the USA could not afford to lose allies.

I urge you to take issue with McCarthy and make it stick. People in high and low places see in him a potential Hitler ... That he could get away with what he already has in America has made some of them wonder whether our concept of democratic government and the rights of individuals is really different from those of the communist and fascists.

Tasks

1. *Why was McCarthy able to win the support of many US people so quickly?*

(Remember the tips given on page 80 about answering a 'Why?' question.)

2. *Sources B and C are from Republicans. Why do you think that the two sources differ so much?*

3. *Look at Source D. Why was Reed so concerned about McCarthy?*

4. *Working in a group, put forward a list of reasons why McCarthyism seemed to contradict the basic ideals of a free and open society.*

Why did McCarthyism fade away?

The role of President Eisenhower

Even though McCarthy was a Republican, this did not prevent him from attacking his own party after the presidential election. The new president, Eisenhower, had done little to challenge him and McCarthy seemed to think he could attack anyone with impunity. He objected to President Eisenhower's choice of ambassador to the Soviet Union (Charles Bohlen) but was overruled by a special Senate committee.

Eisenhower and his government dealt with the communist threat in its own way. A Federal Loyalty Programme, similar to that of Truman's, was introduced and then the Communist Control Act was passed. This limited the legal rights of the party and made membership extremely difficult.

The role of the army

McCarthy sealed his own fate when he began to cast doubts about the security of the army. His investigations were televised from April to June 1954 and, in these, the American public saw for the first time the true nature of the man. He never produced any hard evidence and relied on bluster and bluff. Furthermore, McCarthy was very aggressive in his questioning of witnesses – some felt he bullied in his cross-examinations. The army attorney, Joseph Welch, approached the hearing in a calm and measured manner in contrast to McCarthy. The claims against the army were seen to be unfounded and McCarthy himself now faced challenges.

The role of the media

There had already been a television programme in March 1954 which condemned McCarthy. The acclaimed journalist, Ed Murrow (see Source A), produced a programme based almost entirely on McCarthy's words and this showed clearly the shabby nature of all the baseless claims.

> **Source A:** **Ed Murrow, a leading American journalist, 9 March 1954, attacking McCarthyism**
>
> *The line between investigating and persecuting is a very fine one and … [McCarthy] has stepped over it repeatedly. This is no time for those who oppose him to keep quiet.*

Other journalists began to attack McCarthy (see Source B) and, at last, those who had feared him now had the confidence to express their views openly.

> **Source B:** **Louisville Courier-Journal, 1954, attacking McCarthyism**
>
> *In this long, degrading distortion of the democratic process McCarthy has shown himself to be evil and unmatched in malice.*

McCarthy's fall

In December 1954, McCarthy was publicly reprimanded by the Senate for:

- contempt of a Senate elections sub-committee
- abuse of certain senators
- insults to the Senate during the very hearings which condemned him.

The vote was 67–22 in favour of censuring him. (Only one **Democrat** did not vote for reprimand – John F Kennedy.)

McCarthy then lost the chairmanship of the Committee on Operations of the Senate and this signalled the end of his power. For many, his death in 1957 was not a time for mourning.

Senator McCarthy in a tight corner. What is the message that the cartoonist is trying to get across about McCarthy?

Tasks

1. *Draw a pro-McCarthy poster about the spread of communism in the USA.*

2. *Why did McCarthyism cease to have such a hold on the American people?*

Examination practice

Question 1 – 'In what ways … ?'

In what ways was McCarthy able to maintain the fear of communism? (5 marks)

How to answer

There are often questions in Section (a) of the exam paper which begin – 'In what ways did … ?' Such a question should be straightforward:

- Check to see how many marks are to be awarded – normally five or seven – and then begin to plan your answer.
- Jot down key points and make sure you can organise them into their order of importance.
- Begin the answer with the actual words within the question – this will ensure that the focus is clear and sharp.

What were McCarthyism's effects?

McCarthy's brief time as 'Communist-finder General' had divided the USA and his influence lived on after him.

- The words 'red', 'pinko', 'commie' and 'lefty' became synonymous with someone who was politically unsound, unpatriotic and therefore a threat to the USA.
- McCarthy had created a climate of fear, and with the Cold War still raging in the 1950s it was difficult for people to overcome their fears. There was much spying on neighbours, and government films encouraged people to expose anyone who was thought to have communist sympathies.
- Anyone who sought to change the USA, for example bringing in civil rights for black Americans, was seen as a communist.
- The hatred of communism never died away.

Abroad, the communist threat did seem to have diminished a little and the world situation seemed

> **Armistice**
> An agreement for a temporary end to hostilities.
>
> *Key Term*

to be changing gradually after 1953. Stalin had died and his replacement, Khrushchev, was prepared to improve East–West relations. An **armistice** had helped to bring hostilities in the Korean War to a close – communism seemed to have been contained.

Nevertheless, the climate of fear still existed within the USA and can best be seen in Arthur Miller's play *The Crucible* (1953). Though written at the height of the hysteria, the play has never lost popularity. Furthermore, the 1955 film *Invasion of the Body Snatchers* proved to be successful in warning Americans of the dangers of people such as McCarthy.

> **Task**
>
> *What were the effects of McCarthyism on the people of the USA?*

A poster for the 1955 film *Invasion of the Body Snatchers*, which warned of the dangers of McCarthyism. The science fiction film depicted aliens taking over the bodies of humans so that they could not be recognised. Why do you think some people interpreted this film as a warning against communism?

8 Civil rights in the USA, 1941–80

Task

Study the two photographs.

What can you learn from them about attitudes to racial minorities in the USA at this time?

A segregated cinema in the USA, 1943. Notice the barrier dividing the seats.

Japanese-American citizens on route to an internment camp in March 1942. Anxious to show their loyalty to their country, they flash 'victory' signs.

Racial and sexual discrimination was a common feature of everyday life in the USA before the Second World War. Black Americans experienced segregation and discrimination in all walks of life. When war broke out there was increased optimism that things would change. After all, if the USA was fighting fascism and racism, how could it continue to discriminate and deny civil rights to large sections of its population? In the 1960s, black Americans secured full civil rights, but many felt that though they had the law on their side there was still much to do.

This chapter will try to answer the following questions:

- In what ways did the Second World War change attitudes to racial discrimination?
- How did the legal system help to bring change in the 1950s?
- How important was the role of Martin Luther King?
- Why were the sit-ins and freedom riders important?
- What were the key changes of the 1960s?
- Why did the Black Muslim and Black Power movements emerge?

Exam skills

The chapter will focus and give guidance on answering the **key features** style of question. The amount of marks available for this question can be five, seven or ten.

How did the war affect civil rights?

Japanese-Americans

When war broke out, there was general tolerance towards people of German and Italian ancestry within the USA. However, this was not the case with Japanese-Americans. The attack on Pearl Harbor had left a scar on the USA (see page 71) and Japan and its people could not be forgiven. In early 1942, 112,000 Japanese-Americans (more than half of them were American citizens) were moved into internment camps. President Roosevelt signed Executive Order 9066 which authorised the removal of Japanese-Americans from the west coast of the USA.

The use of internment camps was justified on the grounds that these people would commit acts of sabotage and would act as spies for Japan unless they were closely guarded. The contradiction of this policy was that the men were still subject to the **draft** and 8,000 were called up. In fact, 9,000 others actually volunteered to serve in the armed forces.

Although they lost property, civil rights and endured financial and economic hardships in the camps, the Japanese-Americans remained true to the USA.

Women and the war

Task

1. *Study the two photographs of female workers (right and on the following page). What can you learn about employment opportunities for women in the Second World War?*

Key Terms

Battle of the Bulge
Hitler's last assault on allied forces in the West.

Desegregation
Removal of the policy of separation.

Draft
US method of recruitment into the armed forces. It was compulsory for men (youths) who reached the age of eighteen, to serve in the armed forces.

Female workers in the arms industry during the war.

Female workers during the war.

Black Americans

The photograph shows a skilled black American naval worker in 1945.

In the war years, about six million more women joined the workforce and there was a total of 18.5 million women in work by 1945. They were able to secure employment in many occupations. The biggest increase was in industries such as aeroplane manufacture and shipbuilding, where female employment jumped by almost five times.

However, women received as much as 60 per cent less pay than men, and the earnings gap between men and women actually increased during the war. Moreover, there was often a patronising tone given to the work and role of women – those working in war production were called WOWs (Women Ordnance Workers), in the navy they were WAVES (Women Accepted for Volunteer Emergency Service) and in the army WACS (Women's Army Corps).

The war did mean a broadening of opportunities for black American women. The number who worked in domestic service fell from 75 per cent to less than 50 per cent by 1945. Many became nurses but were only permitted to help black American soldiers.

Prejudice still existed against women workers, and it is estimated that about four million women had lost their wartime jobs by the end of 1946.

There were few advances in civil rights during the war. Segregation still existed in the armed forces, where black Americans performed the menial tasks and found promotion difficult. When black soldiers were injured, only blood from black soldiers could be used, many whites felt that to mix blood would 'mongrelise' the USA.

The reaction to this among black soldiers was to push for a 'Double V' campaign – victory for civil rights at home as well as militarily abroad (read pages 74–75 again). Gradually there was change:

- In the air-force, by the end of 1945, 600 black pilots had been trained.
- There were some mixed units in the army during the **Battle of the Bulge** (late 1944).
- **Desegregation** in the navy came in 1946, and the other services in 1948.

Black Americans and employment

The body of Cleo Wright, a black man who was burned by a mob after being taken from the custody of officers, is observed by a crowd in Missouri, 1942. The victim was suspected of attempted rape of a white woman.

Task

2. Study Source A and the photograph above. What can you learn from them about attitudes in the USA to black Americans during the war?

In 1941, Philip Randolph, a leading black American fighting for equality, sought to remove discrimination in the armed forces and the workplace. He organised the March on Washington Movement and used the slogan 'We loyal Americans demand the right to work and fight for our country'. Randolph wanted changes that would help both southern and northern blacks.

Roosevelt feared a huge march on the capital and, in discussion with Randolph, some gains were made for black Americans. Roosevelt issued

Executive Order 8802 which not only stopped discrimination in industrial and government jobs but also set up the Fair Employment Practices Commission (FEPC) (see page 74).

As a result, the numbers of black Americans employed in government service increased from 50,000 to 200,000.

Effects of the war

Awareness of discrimination and its injustice led to a growth in membership of the National Association for the Advancement of Coloured People (NAACP) – from 50,000 to 450,000 by 1945. A new organisation was set up called Congress of Racial Equality in 1942. This used the idea of **sit-ins** at cinemas and restaurants to highlight the issue of segregation – this did lead to the end of this practice in some northern cities.

The issue of civil rights split the Democrats in the 1948 presidential election. Truman was acutely aware of the racial tensions within the USA (see Source B) but he knew that he would have to tread carefully because many of the **Dixiecrats** would vote against any of his reforming measures. He wanted to introduce a civil rights bill, and also put forward an anti-**lynching** bill, but both were rejected by the southern Dixiecrats.

By the end of the decade, those seeking improved civil rights had made only modest gains.

Source B: From a letter by Harry S Truman, 18 August 1948, describing his revulsion at lynching

I am asking for equality of opportunity for all human beings and as long as I stay here, I shall continue that fight. When the mob gangs can take four people and shoot them in the back and everybody in the country is acquainted with who did the shooting and nothing is done about it, that country is in a pretty bad fix …

3. *Was there any progress in civil rights for US citizens in the 1940s? Draw a diagram like the one below.*

- *In the central boxes put 'Japanese-Americans', 'Women' and 'Black Americans'.*

- *In the boxes to the left give reasons why there was progress.*

- *In the boxes to the right give reasons why there was not progress.*

One example has been started for you. This task helps you to assess whether there was any progress in civil rights for the three specified groups.

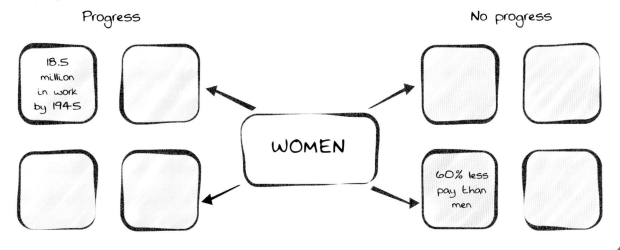

Examination practice

In the examination you will be asked to answer a question which says:

> 'Describe the key features of …'

For this type of 'key features' question, you need to have some knowledge of the subject and you must explain and develop your answer carefully. For example, consider the following question.

Question 1 – key features
Describe the key features of the treatment of the Japanese-Americans in the Second World War.
(5 marks)

How to answer
- Plan your answer: think of the relevant points – the main question word is 'describe' and the topic is treatment of the Japanese-Americans. Therefore, write about:
  - the loss of civil rights
  - the internment camps
  - loss of property
  - men drafted into the army.
- There are only four points but you need to write about each one. You may wish to start by using the words of the question.

Example
'The key feature of the treatment was one of harshness because …'

Question 2 – key features
Describe the key features of the impact of the Second World War on black Americans.
(7 marks)

Now have a go yourself
Tip: this time there are two more marks – try to add more knowledge. Aim to write about half a side of A4 paper.

How did the legal system bring change?

A segregated 'White Only' launderette in the American South.

Segregated water fountains in the American South.

Task

1. *What can you learn about the American South from the two photographs above?*

After the end of the American Civil War in 1865, southern states passed laws to segregate blacks from whites in daily life. These were the 'Jim Crow' laws and the **Supreme Court** had ruled that

Key Terms

Basic human rights
Such as free speech, assumed to belong to all people everywhere.

Militant
Aggressive in support of a cause.

Supreme Court
The highest federal court in the USA consisting of nine judges, chosen by the president, who make sure that the president and congress obey the rules of the Constitution.

if separate conditions for blacks and whites were equal, then segregation was constitutional. This became the 'separate but equal' doctrine and it was to be challenged in the 1950s.

Brown v Topeka, 1954

The first case to challenge segregation did not originate in the South, but in the mid-West state of Kansas. Linda Brown's parents wanted her to attend a neighbourhood school rather than the school for black Americans which was some miles away. Lawyers from NACCP (led by Thurgood Marshall) presented evidence to the Supreme Court. The process took eighteen months and the decision was announced on 17 May 1954. Chief Justice Warren of the Supreme Court said:

> 'We conclude that in the field of public education the doctrine of 'separate but equal' has no place. Separate educational facilities are inherently unequal.'

However, the judgement did not specify how integration should be carried out – apart from a vague notion of 'at the earliest possible speed'. Some areas began to desegregate but others, especially in the South, took deliberate measures to keep separate schools. The Ku Klux Klan began to re-emerge and less **militant** parents joined White Citizens' Councils which aimed to maintain segregation. Over the next two years, southern state legislatures passed more than 450 laws and resolutions which were aimed to prevent the Brown decision being enforced.

In 1956, the University of Alabama refused to accept Authorine Lucy as a student despite a government court order. It was 1963 before black Americans were allowed to study there.

Little Rock High School, 1957

Black American students being escorted into Little Rock High School in 1957.

country which put itself forward as the champion of freedom and equality.

Eisenhower had to act. He used the National Guard and federal troops to protect the black students for the rest of the school year. Despite the President's intervention, Faubus closed all Arkansas schools the following year, simply to prevent integration.

Many white and most black students had no schooling for a year.

Schools in Arkansas re-opened in 1959 following a Supreme Court ruling.

Why was Little Rock significant?

- It involved the President, thus demonstrating that civil rights was an issue which could no longer be ignored.
- It demonstrated that states would be over-ruled by the federal government when necessary.
- The demonstrations were seen on television and in newspapers across the world. It did the USA no good to be seen as an oppressive nation when it was criticising the communist countries for not allowing their citizens **basic human rights**.
- Many US citizens saw, for the first time, the racial hatred that existed in the southern states.

The crisis at Little Rock eventually forced President Eisenhower to intervene in a forceful manner. After the Brown decision, Little Rock High School, Arkansas decided to allow nine black students to enrol there. The nine, led by Elizabeth Eckford, tried to enrol but were prevented by the Governor, Orval Faubus, who ordered state National Guardsmen to block their entry. The following day (4 September 1957), the National Guard were removed by order of Faubus and the nine students ran the gauntlet of a vicious white crowd – by midday, the students went home under police guard because their safety could not be guaranteed.

Press and television coverage in the USA and across the world was a serious embarrassment to a

Tasks

2. *Why do you think that education played such an important part in the quest for civil rights in the 1950s?*

3. *Were Brown v Topeka and Little Rock important in winning improved civil rights? Answer by constructing a balance sheet:*

	Yes, because . . .	No, because . . .
Brown v Topeka		
Little Rock		

How important was the Montgomery Bus Boycott?

Source A: **Verse sung by Montgomery bus boycotters, 1955–56**

Ain't gonna ride them buses no more,
Ain't gonna ride no more,
Why don't all the white folk know
That I ain't gonna ride no more.

From the song, what do you think the bus boycott was about?

Rosa Parks being fingerprinted after her arrest.

The Montgomery Bus Boycott, 1955–57, is often viewed as the defining protest of black Americans. Peaceful protesting, the use of the economic weapon (almost bankrupting the bus company) and the powerful eloquence of Martin Luther King, secured a victory which reverberated around the USA.

Key features of the Boycott

- Segregation on public transport in Alabama was the norm.
- On buses, black Americans had to give up their seats to whites if the vehicle was becoming full and were also unable to sit in seats marked for whites.
- Rosa Parks was asked by a bus driver to give up her seat to a white man. She refused and was subsequently arrested.
- Parks was a respectable member of her community and had also been a secretary of her local NAACP branch (National Association for the Advancement of Coloured People). Local civil rights leaders decided to build a case around her to protest against segregation in transport.
- A boycott was called for and within 48 hours, 35,000 leaflets were printed and distributed encouraging black Americans not to use the buses in Montgomery. The boycott was scheduled to last for one day – it ended after almost 400.

- The Montgomery Improvement Association (MIA) was set up to co-ordinate activities and a local minister, Martin Luther King Jr., led it.
- King's house was firebombed and 88 black community leaders were arrested for conspiring to boycott.
- Taxi firms owned by black Americans helped to take people to work.
- Car-pooling was organised to take as many people to work as possible.
- The bus company soon began to lose money.
- Throughout the boycott, there were appeals to the Supreme Court challenging segregation on buses. On 20 December 1956, the Court declared that segregation was unconstitutional and the boycott was called off.
- A peaceful approach had secured a significant victory and one which showed that the black Americans were able to organise themselves.

The emergence of Martin Luther King Jr.

Biography Martin Luther King Jr., 1929–1968

1929 Born January 15
1951 Graduated from Crozer Theological
      College with a degree in theology
1953 Married Coretta Scott
1955 Completed PhD from Boston University
1955 Led Montgomery Bus Boycott
1957 Formed and led Southern Christian
      Leadership Conference
1963 'I have a dream' speech. Voted 'Man of
      the year' by *Time* Magazine
1964 Winner of the Nobel Peace Prize
1968 April 4, assassinated in Memphis

King speaks to reporters outside the Montgomery County
Court House before the opening of his trial, in March
1956. He was the first of ninety African-Americans
indicted on boycotting charges involving the Montgomery
buses.

King was the son of a Baptist minister and grew
up in a comfortable middle-class home in Atlanta,
Georgia. As a teenager he spoke in his father's
church and demonstrated that he had a gift for
popular speaking.

He had been minister at the Dexter Avenue
Baptist Church, Montgomery, for less than a year
when the boycott began. He was chosen as leader
of the MIA because of this – he had not been there
long enough to become too close to any particular
local organisation. During the dispute, he
organised the car pools and when he was prevented
from taking out local insurance for the vehicles, he
went as far as using Lloyd's of London.

His energy and enthusiasm were unbounded in
the boycott and he had the ability to inspire those
who worked with him. His idea of using non-
violent tactics was similar to those of Gandhi in
India and soon there were many civil rights
activists keen to follow King in the quest for
equality.

Following the boycott, King was instrumental in
setting up the Southern Christian Leadership
Conference and became its president in 1957. He
was now one of the leading figures in the civil
rights movement.

The Southern Christian Leadership Conference

Formed in 1957 by King and two other leading
civil rights campaigners, its aim was to co-
ordinate and assist local organisations in
working towards equality for black Americans.

Examination practice

1. Explain why the Montgomery Bus Boycott
   was important for black Americans in the
   1950s.   (5 marks)

(Remember the tips given on page 80 about
answering a 'Why?' question.)

2. Describe the key features of the
   Montgomery Bus Boycott.   (10 marks)

(See page 91 on answering a 'key features'
question. However, this time the question has
ten marks. Plan your answer carefully and be
prepared to write almost one page of A4 paper.
Take the examiner through the key features in
sequence and at all times focus on the key
points. How it started – what happened – how
it finished.)

Why were the protests important?

Greensboro, North Carolina, 1960

Just as King was emerging as a powerful force in the civil rights movement, events in North Carolina showed the extent to which students would go to fight segregation. A sit-in was held at the Greensboro branch of Woolworth's – four black students from a local college demanded to be served at a whites-only lunch counter and, on being refused, remained seated at the counter until the shop closed. The next day they were accompanied by 27 more students and the day after 80 more. By the fifth day there were 300. The shop agreed to make a few concessions but the students later resumed their protests – some were now arrested for trespass. The students then boycotted any shop in Greensboro which had segregated lunch counters. Sales immediately dropped and segregation ended. For the second time the economic weapon was used successfully.

Consequences of the Greensboro sit-in

- By April 1960, students in 78 communities across the South had held sit-ins.
- 2,000 protestors were arrested.
- By September 1961, it was estimated that there had been about 70,000 black and white students who had used the tactic of the sit-in.

Key Terms

Congress of Racial Equality

Established in 1942 by James Farmer. CORE was the first organisation in the USA to use the tactic of sit-ins.

Enfranchise

To give an individual the right to vote.

Segregationists

Those who believed in the policy of separation of races.

SNCC

Student Non-violent Co-ordinating Committee – founded by students at Shaw University, North Carolina. Its aim was to attack examples of discrimination and by peaceful methods, demand equality for black Americans.

- Variations on a theme developed – there were 'kneel-ins' to integrate churches, 'wade-ins' at beaches, 'read-ins' at libraries and 'sleep-ins' at motel lobbies.
- 810 towns and cities had desegregated public areas by the end of 1961.
- Publicity was gained for the civil rights movement when television showed the non-violence of the protestors in face of some violent white opponents.

A sit-in at a 'whites-only' lunch counter in Jackson, Mississippi. What can you learn about the attitudes of the crowd in the photograph?

Freedom riders

The Supreme Court decided in December 1960 that all bus stations and terminals that served interstate travellers should be integrated. The **Congress of Racial Equality** (CORE) wanted to test that decision by employing the tactic of the freedom ride. If there was continued failure to carry out the law, CORE would be able to show that narrow-mindedness and racism still existed in the Southern states.

The first of the freedom rides began in May 1961, when thirteen CORE volunteers left Washington DC by bus to travel to New Orleans. There was little trouble on the first part of the journey – the black Americans used whites-only facilities to ensure integration was taking place. However, at Anniston, Alabama, a bus was attacked and burnt.

> **Source A** **From an interview with James Peck who rode the first freedom bus. Here he is describing what happened when he arrived in Anniston in May 1961**
>
> *As Charles Person and I entered the white waiting room and approached the lunch counter, we were grabbed and pushed outside into an alleyway. As soon as we got into the alleyway and were out of sight of the onlookers in the waiting room, six men started swinging at me with fists and pipes. Five others attacked Charles. Within seconds, I was unconscious.*

In Birmingham, there was no protection for the riders and they were attacked by an angry mob – the police chief (Bull Connor) had given most of the police the day off. Events at Jackson, Mississippi, forced the new president, Kennedy, to intervene. Kennedy secured a promise from the state senator that there would be no mob violence. However, when the riders arrived in Jackson, they were immediately arrested when they tried to use the whites-only waiting room.

The riders continued throughout the summer and more than 300 of them were imprisoned in Jackson alone. Attacks on them by the Ku Klux Klan increased. The Attorney General, Robert Kennedy, did not wish to see the situation escalate and was hoping that he would not have to send in US Marshals to enforce the law. Violence was avoided in Mississippi and Kennedy was able to announce on 22 September that there would be no further challenges to de-segregating interstate travel.

Voter Education Project

The freedom rides caused Robert Kennedy to fear violent confrontations between the black civil rights groups and white **segregationists**. He felt that if more black Americans voted, then they would be able to have a greater say in such issues as housing and education. Kennedy met various groups and the Voter Education Project was set up. The Project was staffed mainly by members of the Student Non-violent Co-ordinating Committee (**SNCC**) and they spent much time with eligible voters showing them how to register and overcome the barriers which were placed in front of them – for example, the mathematical questions which were impossible to answer.

The project did result in many black Americans being **enfranchised** but many were refused the right to vote on dubious grounds. The SNCC workers were subject to harassment – in Georgia, several churches were bombed, workers were beaten up and some shot. Those who did register and voted were sometimes evicted from their land, sacked from their job and refused **credit**. The SNCC felt betrayed because they thought Kennedy would protect them – both President Kennedy and Robert Kennedy were of the opinion that the local police should protect the SNCC workers.

> ### Tasks
>
> 1. *What is meant by the term: freedom rider? (Remember the tips you were given on page 76 about answering this type of question.)*
>
> 2. *Prepare a one-minute talk to explain why you support the method of the sit-in.*
>
> 3. *Construct a balance sheet for freedom rides and the Voter Education Project – showing how they were successful/unsuccessful.*
>
> 4. *Describe the part played by President Kennedy and Robert Kennedy in improving civil rights in the early 1960s.*

What were the changes in the 1960s?

The Meredith case

James Meredith (centre) entering Mississippi University, Oxford, Mississippi, 1962.

In June 1962, the Supreme Court upheld a federal court decision to force Mississippi University to accept James Meredith. The university did not want any black students and Meredith was prevented from registering. In his first major involvement in civil rights, President Kennedy sent in federal marshals to escort Meredith to the campus. There were riots and two people were killed and 70 were wounded. Soldiers had to remain on the campus until he received his degree – three years later.

Source A: Part of Bob Dylan's song 'Oxford Town'. Dylan was singing about the Meredith case

He went down to Oxford Town
Guns and clubs followed him down
All because his face was brown
Better get away from Oxford Town
Oxford Town in the afternoon
Ev'rybody singin' a sorrowful tune
Two men died 'neath the Mississippi moon
Somebody better investigate soon.

Birmingham, Alabama, 1963

The civil rights issue seemed to explode in 1963. Although the sit-ins had had some success, there was still no federal law which made southern states integrate their public facilities. In order to avoid de-segregating its parks, playgrounds, swimming pools and golf courses Birmingham simply closed them all.

The Southern Christian Leadership Conference sought to challenge the city with Project C – 'Confrontation' – which would use the tactic of sit-ins to press for de-segregation at lunch counters. It was hoped that the demonstrations would achieve maximum publicity across the USA. They did. Martin Luther King was arrested and jailed for defying a ban on marches – he was arrested on Good Friday and during his short stay in prison, he wrote 'Letter from Birmingham Jail' (see Source B).

Source B: Part of King's 'Letter from Birmingham Jail'

*For years, I have heard the word 'Wait!' It rings in the ear of every **Negro** with piercing familiarity. This 'Wait!' has almost always meant 'Never'. We must come to see that justice too long delayed is justice denied.*

The situation worsened on his release from jail. It was decided that children and students would be used in the demonstrations, and this seemed to change the police's methods. Bull Connor, the Birmingham police chief, allowed his men to set dogs on the protesters and he then called in the fire department to use powerful water hoses.

Police dogs attacking civil rights demonstrators in Birmingham, Alabama, 1963.

Connor placed almost 2,000 demonstrators in jail. Television witnessed the events, and images of them were seen not only across the USA but also all over the world.

It was at this stage that President Kennedy became involved – he sent a representative to mediate between the parties and hopefully find a solution. Desegregation was eventually introduced in the city. A consequence of the violence was Kennedy's decision to bring in a Civil Rights Bill. (See Source C.)

On that same day, 11 June 1963, Medgar Evers, leader of the Mississippi National Association for the Advancement of Coloured People, was shot dead in Jackson by a white sniper.

Source C: From a speech made on television by President Kennedy on 11 June 1963, about the need to improve civil rights for black Americans

We preach freedom around the world, and we mean it … But are we to say to the world – and much more importantly to one another – that this is the land of the free except for the Negroes? We face a moral crisis as a country and a people. It cannot be met by repressive police action. It cannot be left to increased demonstrations in our streets. It is a time to act in Congress and in our daily lives.

Tasks

1. *What message did the death of Medgar Evans and the image of dogs attacking demonstrators send to people of the USA and the world?*

2. *Explain why President Kennedy had become involved in the civil rights issue by 1963.*

Use the information and sources on these two pages to help you answer the question. You must plan the answer carefully – it is important that you are able to select information, make judgements and present a clear case. Cite the sources, use evidence to support your answer and ensure that you have addressed the question.

Why were King's campaigns important?

The March on Washington, August 1963

Martin Luther King leading civil rights demonstrators on the March to Washington DC. Why do you think such photographs became important in the campaign for civil rights?

Source A: From King's speech at Washington DC, 28 August 1963

I have a dream one day that on the red hills of Georgia, sons of former slaves and sons of former slave owners will be able to sit down together at the table of brotherhood …

I have a dream that my four little children will one day live in a nation where they will not be judged by the colour of their skin but by the content of their character. I have a dream today!

After Birmingham, the civil rights groups wanted to maintain the impetus and some sought to commemorate the centenary of the freeing of the slaves. The idea of a huge march on Washington DC was put forward and the key groups (NAACP, CORE, SNCC and SCLC) took part.

The march initially began as a cry for jobs, but its aims broadened to cover the whole of the civil rights movement. There was naturally a demand for the passage of Kennedy's civil rights bill. King was keen to have the march because he knew that there were those in the movement who felt that progress was slow and who might drift towards violence if the high profile was not sustained.

When the march took place, there were about 250,000 demonstrators (it has been estimated that there were around 80,000 white supporters) – the organisers had expected less than half this figure. King was the final speaker of the day and his speech has now become part of the lore of struggle for civil rights (see Source A).

King's hopes seemed illusory because in September 1963, four black children were killed in a bomb attack while attending Sunday school in Birmingham.

Civil Rights Legislation

Kennedy's Civil Rights Bill went through its first stages in November 1963, but his death delayed its progress. The new President, Johnson, was able to push the bill through the **House of Representatives** and the Senate ensuring that those Southern Democrats who opposed the Bill would be counter-balanced by Republicans. Johnson had been in high-level politics since 1938 and he needed all his skills to persuade and cajole the Republicans to vote with him. There were, of course, those in Congress who voted sympathetically for the Bill following Kennedy's assassination. (See the box on the Act, on the next page.)

Selma and the Voting Rights Act, 1965

The Civil Rights Act did not mean that black Americans could vote, so King and his colleagues decided to force the issue by embarking on another non-violent campaign.

The town of Selma, Alabama was to be the battleground as there were only 383 black

> ### The Civil Rights Act, 1964
> ### (See also Chapter 9, page 114.)
>
> - Segregation in hotels, motels, restaurants, lunch counters and theatres was banned.
>
> - The Act placed the responsibility on the federal government to bring cases to court where discrimination still occurred.
>
> - Any business engaged in business with the government would be monitored to ensure there was no discrimination.
>
> - The Fair Employment Practices Committee (see page 74) was established on a permanent basis.

American voters who had been able to register out of a possible 15,000. The sheriff of Selma, Jim Clark, had a reputation to match that of Bull Connor in Birmingham. King was hoping for a brutal reaction to his demonstrations because he knew that the press and television would again highlight the continued bigotry of the South.

There were two months of attempts to register black voters and two months of rejections. King and his followers were subjected to beatings and arrests. One demonstrator was murdered. It was decided to hold a march from Selma to the state capital, Birmingham, in order to present to Governor Wallace a petition asking for voting rights. Wallace banned the march but King was determined to take his supporters and lobby the Governor.

The march was stopped on the Edmund Pettus Bridge and the marchers were attacked by Sheriff Clark's men and state troopers. The marchers faced tear gas, horses and clubs and were forced to return to Selma. This became known as 'Bloody Sunday' and forced President Johnson's hand. A second march took place two days later and King turned the marchers back – he had agreed with Johnson that he would avoid violent confrontation with Clark again.

Public opinion across the USA was firmly behind King and the civil rights movement and on 15 March, President Johnson promised to put forward a bill that would enfranchise black Americans. Eventually, it was agreed that the march from Selma to Birmingham would go ahead if it was peaceful. King led more than 25,000 on 21 March – this was the biggest ever that had been seen in the South.

The Voting Rights Act, 1965

The success of the march created an atmosphere of optimism and in the summer, President Johnson introduced the Voting Rights Bill. The Act:

- ended literacy tests
- ensured federal agents could monitor registration – and step in if it was felt there was discrimination.

By the end of 1965, 250,000 black Americans had registered (one-third had been assisted by government monitors who checked that the law was being followed). A further 750,000 registered by the end of 1968. Furthermore, the number of elected black representatives increased rapidly after the Act.

King's policy of non-violence appeared to have worked. There was widespread support and sympathy from white Americans and there had been two key pieces of legislation which had removed discrimination and **disenfranchisement**. However, other groups were emerging that opposed King's idea of non-violence.

> ### Voting Rights
>
> In 1870, by the Fifteenth Amendment, male black Americans were given the right to vote. However, some states disenfranchised them by such means as unfair taxation and literacy tests. The literacy tests were not a test of reading and writing, they asked difficult arithmetic and cultural questions which most people would have found impossible.

> ### Tasks
>
> 1. *Describe the key features of King's methods in the years 1960–63.*
> *(Remember how to approach this question by looking at page 91 in this chapter.)*
>
> 2. *Working in groups, prepare a presentation to show that King was successful/unsuccessful in achieving his aims in the years 1960–63. Remember to quote from the sources and/or explain the points you make.*

Why did Black Power emerge?

Malcolm X and the Black Muslims

For some in the civil rights movement, progress had been painfully slow and a feeling grew that King's methods would never bring equality in politics and equality of opportunity in life. A group which had never accepted King's ideas was the Nation of Islam (or Black Muslims) – its supporters openly sought **separatism**. Members rejected their slave surnames and called themselves 'X'.

Nation of Islam

Founded in 1931 by Wallace Fard and led by Elijah Muhammad after 1934. The Nation of Islam did not teach the orthodox Islamic faith, and preached that Christianity would be destroyed.

The most famous member of the Nation of Islam was Malcolm X, and his brilliant oratory skills helped to increase membership to about 100,000. He had a tremendous influence on young urban black Americans. He felt that violence could be justified not only for self-defence but also as a means to secure a separate black nation. However, after a visit to Mecca, he changed his views and left the Black Muslims to set up the Organisation of Afro-American Unity to promote closer ties between Africans and African-Americans. He pushed to end racial discrimination in the USA, but this brought him enemies and he was assassinated by three black Muslims in February 1965.

Separatism
Keeping races apart.

Key Term

Malcolm X addresses a rally on May 14, 1963, in support of desegregation in Birmingham, Alabama. How does he come across in this photograph?

Black Power

Despite the civil rights laws, many young black Americans were frustrated, and those who lived in the ghettos felt anger at the high rates of unemployment, continuing discrimination and poverty which they experienced. In August 1965, this frustration exploded into a major riot in the Watts district of Los Angeles. The riot caused about $40 million of damage. There were riots across the USA's major cities in the two following summers. Huge numbers of rioters were involved – 30,000 in the Watts area and, in the Detroit riot of 1967, 7,000 people were arrested. There were more than one hundred riots which saw 130 people killed and damage totalling more than $700 million.

The frustration experienced by young black Americans began to boil over. Like many young people across the world at this time their impatience expressed itself in a militant and aggressive manner.

As the riots raged, the Black Power movement emerged. Stokely Carmichael and others in the SNCC wanted blacks to take responsibility for their own lives and rejected white help. They wanted blacks to have pride in their heritage and adopted the slogan 'Black is beautiful'. Furthermore, Carmichael attacked the involvement of the USA in the Vietnam War.

Black Panther Party for Self Defence

This party emerged in California and was founded by Huey Newton and Bobby Seale. The Black Panthers wanted full employment, good housing and adequate education and were prepared to use revolutionary means to achieve them. The Panthers wore uniforms and were prepared to use weapons, training members in their use. By the end of 1968, they had 5,000 members. However, internal divisions and the events of 1969, which saw 27 Panthers killed and 700 injured in confrontations with the police, saw support diminish. The party disbanded in 1982.

King knew that he had lost some influence among the black Americans since 1965. He found it difficult to compete with the more radical movements and in his speeches he tried to keep to his message of old (see Source B).

Looters being arrested after the riots in Newark, 1967.

Tasks

1. *Write a speech for a SNCC meeting. In it explain why you have now rejected King's approach and agree with Stokely Carmichael's approach.*

2. *Describe the key features of the Black Panther Party.*
(Remember how to approach this type of question – see page 91.)

3. *Do some further individual research on Malcolm X, Huey Newton and the Nation of Islam.*

The Kerner Report

The riots of 1965–67 caused President Johnson and his advisers to look into the factors behind them. The Black Power movement had made it clear that equality of opportunity did not exist and the Kerner Report (1968) stated that racism was deeply embedded in American society. The report not only highlighted the economic issues faced by black Americans but also the 'systematic police bias and brutality'.

The Kerner Report recommended sweeping federal initiatives which would mean increased expenditure. Following the election of President Nixon later that year, the report was largely ignored.

The assassination of King

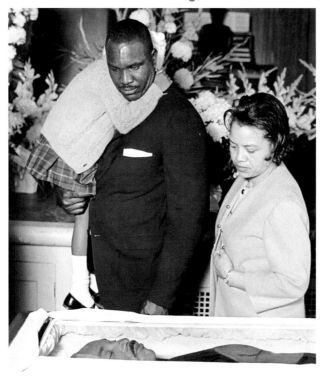

Martin Luther King's body lying in state, 1968.

On 4 April 1968, Martin Luther King was in Memphis. He was visiting Memphis because he was supporting black refuse collectors who were striking for equal treatment with their white co-workers. This seemed to indicate that social and economic issues were becoming increasingly important to the civil rights movement. However, King was finding it more difficult to control his followers who could not always keep to his principle of non-violence. King was assassinated on that same day in Memphis. James Earl Ray, a white racist, was arrested and jailed for the crime, but there is still doubt over whether he was the real killer.

On his death, there was a final outburst of rioting across the country. Forty-six people died, more than 3,000 were injured in violent clashes and demonstrations across more than one hundred cities. This was a great irony – it seemed as if King's whole work and life had been for nothing.

The year of 1968 did seem to be the end of an era. There was a new president, Nixon, the Vietnam War had begun to dominate the domestic scene and the student movement also took centre stage (see Chapter 9).

Task

4. Write an epitaph for Martin Luther King. (An epitaph is usually to be found on someone's gravestone, summarising briefly their achievement in life.)

How extensive were the changes?

Source A: Graph showing elected black officials, 1965–85

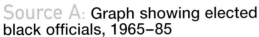

Source B: Black American and national unemployment figures in the years, 1960–80

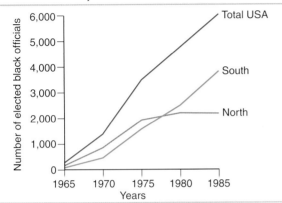

Source C: From an article about civil rights in a British History magazine for GCSE students

There were definite improvements in the quality of life for many of America's disadvantaged; in 1965, 19 per cent of black Americans earned the average wage, by 1967, this had risen to 27 per cent; in 1960, the average educated age of a black American was 10.8, by 1967 this had increased to 12.2.

Source D: Table showing registered voters in certain states in the USA, 1969

State	Percentage of white people registered	Percentage of black people registered
Alabama	94.6	61.3
Arkansas	81.6	77.9
Florida	94.2	67.0
Georgia	88.5	60.4
Louisiana	87.1	60.8
Mississippi	89.8	66.5
North Carolina	70.4	50.7
South Carolina	71.5	54.6
Tennessee	92.0	92.1
Texas	61.8	73.1
Virginia	78.7	58.9
USA as a whole	80.4	64.8

Source E: Table to show percentage of people living in poverty in the USA in the years, 1959–68

	1959	1963	1966	1968
Whole population	22.4	19.5	14.7	12.8
Whites	18.1	15.3	11.3	10.0
Non-whites	56.2	51.0	39.8	33.5

Task

Look back over the whole chapter and the sources on this page. The focus of your reading should be to examine how civil rights were gained and if the changes brought any positive gains for black Americans. Then, using the sources on this page, construct a balance sheet, for example:

Change	Positive gain because ...	No difference because ...
Fall in number living in poverty (Source E).	Removal of poverty can lead to better opportunities in education.	Still substantially larger amount of black people living in poverty than whites.

Examination practice

In Chapter 9 (page 116) there is thorough guidance about the construction of an essay. Here you are given some initial tips which, if acted upon, will mean that you present a clear and explained response. This is what the examiner is looking for – s/he does not want information to be jumbled or contain irrelevant information – the answer must be focused, direct and must clearly address the question.

- Look at the dates in the question and work out why they have been selected. They give you a framework, e.g. *1954 – first key change and Voting Rights is the climax of King's work.*
- Focus on the topic and which part of it is being examined, e.g. *civil rights for black Americans only.*
- Ensure you target the key question words, for example 'why', 'how', 'in what ways' and then look for the key target words, for example 'improve', 'change', 'develop', 'effects', etc. Use the target word in your answer – this should mean that you are answering the question.
- Look at the four pieces of information you have been given. Can you write several sentences about them? They will assist you through the question.
- Add any additional information that you know about the topic – provided that it expands the four points, thus remaining relevant at all times. Try to use link words/phrases such as 'furthermore', 'in addition', 'moreover', 'consequently'. These will lend a more mature approach to the answer.

Now answer these questions

1. In what ways did civil rights improve for black Americans in the years 1954 to 1965?

You may refer to the following in your answer:
- 1954 Brown v Topeka
- 1957 Little Rock High School
- 1964 Civil Rights Act
- 1965 Voting Rights Act. (15 marks)

2. Explain why black Americans gained improved civil rights in the years 1945 to 1965.

You may refer to the following in your answer:
- The impact of the Second World War
- The role of President Eisenhower
- The role of Martin Luther King
- The role of Presidents Kennedy and Johnson. (15 marks)

9

The 'New Frontier' and the 'Great Society'

A still from the footage of the assassination of President Kennedy, 22 November 1963.

The assassination of President John F Kennedy in 1963 remains one of the most remembered events of the twentieth century. Indeed, those old enough to remember it always seem to know where they were and what they were doing when they heard of Kennedy's death. It has led to a host of conspiracy theories about who assassinated him and for what reasons.

Kennedy's personal life and period as president continues to fascinate and divide historians. To some he was a breath of fresh air, who greatly changed US society and politics. Others believe his achievements have been exaggerated. He is one of the great 'what ifs' in history. What would he have achieved had he not been assassinated? Because of Kennedy's reputation many have given little credit to the achievements of Lyndon B Johnson, his successor as president. This chapter will try to answer the following questions:

- What was meant by the 'New Frontier'?
- What were the main policies of the New Frontier and how successful were they?
- What opposition was there towards the New Frontier?
- What was meant by the 'Great Society'?
- What changes were brought about by the Great Society?
- Who achieved the most, Kennedy or Johnson?

Exam skills

You will be shown how to plan and answer the ten-mark essay question in Section (b) of Paper 1. This could be a causation, consequence, key features or change essay.

What was meant by the 'New Frontier'?

'We stand at the edge of a New Frontier – the frontier of unknown opportunities and beliefs – a frontier of unfulfilled hopes and dreams … [The New Frontier would deal with] unsolved problems of peace and war, unconquered pockets of ignorance and prejudice, unanswered questions of poverty and surplus.'

This is an extract from Kennedy's acceptance speech as President, in 1960, in which he first mentioned the 'New Frontier'. At first it was simply a slogan to try to unite and inspire the American people and get them behind him. However, it became a programme of reform and change in which Kennedy hoped to make the US a fairer society by giving equal civil rights to all blacks, and by helping people to better themselves.

He called it the 'New Frontier' to make people feel excited and try to reduce opposition to his reforms. Above all he wanted to make the USA a fairer and better place and he asked Americans to join him in being 'New Frontiersmen'.

Spin doctors

Key Term

A relatively recent term, referring to the media people employed to provide a positive image of a government or an individual.

Biography — John F Kennedy (JFK), 1917–63

John Fitzgerald was born into a wealthy Massachusetts family. His father was ambassador to Britain. He was educated at Harvard University and, during the Second World War, served in the US navy when he was badly wounded and decorated for his bravery.

After the war, he entered politics, being elected a **Democratic** congressman in 1947 and, five years later, elected to the US Senate. In 1960 the Democrats chose him to run for president and he narrowly defeated the Republican candidate, Richard M Nixon to become the youngest ever US President.

Before becoming President, Kennedy had written two best-selling books including *Profiles in Courage*, 1953, which was about American politicians who risked their lives to stand up for what they believed in.

Senator John F Kennedy in Seattle on the first day of his presidential campaign, in 1959.

Changes in government

Kennedy also made major changes to central government to ensure that the 'New Frontier' was carried out. For example, he gathered together a team of the brightest young experts from the USA's universities, most of whom had never worked for the government before, including the Secretary for Defence, Robert McNamara. These were known as the Brains Trust. Kennedy hoped that because they were young and fresh, they would come up with new ideas for tackling the problems of the USA.

Others, including Kennedy's vice-president, Lyndon B Johnson, were not so keen. He feared that their lack of experience in politics might handicap any changes they suggested.

What was the Kennedy 'image'?

A typical family image of the Kennedys at a White House reception, 8 February 1961.

The government **spin doctors** of the early 1960s, created an image of Kennedy which many fully accepted until well after his assassination. He was portrayed as the young, faithful, happily married family man with a beautiful wife, Jackie. The two were frequently seen in public together and were more popular than film stars.

In reality this was not the case. The Kennedys were not a happy family. President Kennedy had many affairs including those with Marilyn Monroe, a famous Hollywood star, and the girlfriend of a Mafia boss. Some even suspected that the Mafia blackmailed Kennedy over this and prevented him from taking action against organised crime in the USA.

Tasks

1. *What was meant by the 'New Frontier'? (Can you remember how to do this type of question? If not, refer to page 76.)*

2. *Look again at the brief biography of Kennedy (page 108). Do some of your own research, possibly on the Internet, to find out more about his career before he became president. Imagine you are one of Kennedy's 'spin doctors'.*

• *What could you use in his earlier career to further improve his image?*

• *Give an example of how you would use it.*

What were the New Frontier's policies?

Kennedy is one of the great 'what ifs' in history. What would he have achieved had he not been assassinated?

The main measures

Kennedy's New Frontier policies covered three main areas – civil rights, the economy and social measures.

Civil rights

Kennedy aimed to achieve equality for black Americans:

- He appointed five federal judges, including Thurgood Marshall (see Biography). Marshall was a leading civil rights activist and his appointment showed how committed Kennedy was to this issue.
- He threatened legal action against the state of Louisiana for refusing to fund schools which were not segregated.
- In October 1962, he sent 23,000 government troops to ensure that just one black student, James Meredith, could study at the University of Mississippi.
- He threatened to evict the Washington Redskins football team from their stadium which was funded by the federal or central government, unless they agreed to hire black players.
- By the summer of 1963, Alabama was the only state with a segregated education system.
- He introduced a Civil Rights Bill to Congress in February 1963. This aimed to give black people equality in public housing and education.

However his achievements were very limited.

- He did not play a leading role in the Civil Rights Movement for fear of losing the support of Southern Democrats who opposed civil rights.

The Civil Rights Bill was eventually rejected by Congress.

Key Terms

Boom
Time when the economy is doing well, with a growth in production, exports, employment and often wages.

Minimum wage
The lowest wage per hour that someone can be paid.

Biography Thurgood Marshall, 1908–93

He served as director of the NAACP, National Association for the Advancement of Coloured People (see Chapter 7) from 1940 to 1961 and played an important role in using the Supreme Court to end segregation in education, particularly in the Brown v Topeka case of 1954 (see pages 92–93). In 1965, President Johnson made him Solicitor General. He served on the Supreme Court until 1991.

Economic measures

Kennedy wanted to keep the US economy as the strongest in the world, to 'get the country moving again'.

- He cut **income taxes** to give people more spending money.
- Grants were given to high-tech companies to invest in high-tech equipment to train workers.
- He increased spending on defence and space technology, all of which secured or created jobs, and also promised that the USA would put a man on the moon by the end of the 1960s.
- Finally, he limited prices and wages to ensure inflation did not spiral out of control.

The economy grew quickly and people in work generally prospered.

However, there were limitations:

- There was still unemployment in traditional industries such as coal, iron and steel.
- Unemployment was twice as high among black Americans.
- The **boom** was heavily dependent on government spending.

Social reforms

Kennedy wanted to ensure that poor Americans had the opportunity to help themselves.

- He increased the **minimum wage** from $1 an hour to $1.25.
- His Housing Act enabled people in run-down areas to get loans to improve their housing and local authorities could get money to clear slums.
- His Area Redevelopment Act helped poor communities to get grants or loans to start new businesses.

- The Social Security Act gave greater financial help to the elderly and unemployed. Social security benefits were extended to each child whose father was unemployed.
- The Manpower Development and Training Act retrained the unemployed. A loan of $900 million was authorised to provide work for retrained workers.

Again, there were limitations.

- Slum clearance itself created housing shortages in inner-city areas.
- The minimum wage only helped those who already had a job.
- The poorest people could not afford to pay back the housing loans.
- Medicare, which included free medical care for the old, was thrown out by Congress.

Tasks

1. *Why did Kennedy introduce his 'New Frontier' programme?*

(Remember how to do the five-mark question? If not look back at page 80.)

2. *Use a concept map to show the achievements and limitations of Kennedy's 'New Frontier' programme. Here is a start for you.*

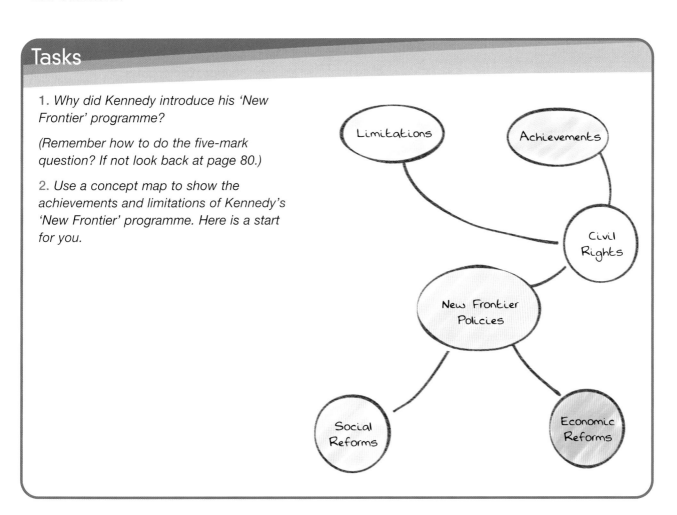

Why was there opposition to Kennedy's measures?

Kennedy faced opposition in Congress to his New Frontier policies.

- His own position as president was not strong as he won a narrow victory in the 1960 presidential campaign.
- Many older members of Congress felt he was too young and inexperienced and distrusted his 'Brains Trust' appointments. Kennedy, himself, was not really interested in domestic politics and made little effort to persuade Congressmen to support his policies.
- Some were suspicious of the radical nature of his New Frontier and the pace of change and saw it as a 'socialist' programme.
- He was the first Catholic president. This, again, created suspicion from the more traditional Protestant politicians.
- The greatest opposition was from Southern Congressmen, even Democrats, members of his own party, who disliked his commitment to civil rights. They feared that equal rights for black people would cost them the votes of whites in the South.
- Kennedy hoped to be re-elected president in 1964 and needed the support of these Southern Democrat Congressmen.
- Some opposed the further extension of the power of federal government and greater central government spending. Many still believed in the values of '**rugged individualism**'.

Kennedy's assassination

On 22 November 1963, Kennedy visited Dallas, Texas, to try to win the support of Southern Democrats for his policies. He was travelling through the city in an open-topped car with his wife Jackie and the Governor of Texas, John Connally, when Kennedy was struck by at least two bullets. He died on his way to hospital. A man, Lee Harvey Oswald, was arrested the same day and accused of his murder. Two days later, Oswald himself was shot by Jack Ruby, a Dallas nightclub owner.

There have been numerous theories put forward about Kennedy's death. Some believe it was part of a Mafia or communist conspiracy and others believe Oswald was innocent.

Whatever the truth, the death shocked the USA and the world and seemed to bring to a premature end a very promising presidency.

Tasks

3. Draw a cartoon character for each of the following with a speech bubble.

- a Southern Congressman

- a keen member of the protestant Church

- an older member of Congress.

Write a speech for each character in the bubbles giving one (or more) of Kennedy's policies that they might oppose with the reason or reasons for their opposition.

4. You are the editor of a British newspaper. You have to produce a front page the day after Kennedy's death. This should include:

- a headline about his death

- an explanation (from what was known at the time) about the circumstances of his death

- an obituary for Kennedy.

What was the 'Great Society'?

Lyndon Johnson was president from 1963 to 1969 and his achievements have often been overlooked or underestimated due to the reputation of Kennedy and the US involvement in the war in Vietnam.

Biography Lyndon Baines Johnson (LBJ), 1908–73

Johnson was born in Texas in 1908 and, as a teacher, saw much of the poverty in his area and became a firm supporter of social reform. In 1937, he was elected to Congress as a Democrat and strongly supported Roosevelt's New Deal.

In 1948, he became a senator and within five years led the Democrats in the Senate. In 1960, he was chosen as Kennedy's vice-presidential candidate because he was experienced and skilled at handling Congress.

He succeeded Kennedy after his assassination in 1963 and, in the following year, was elected President by the widest margin ever achieved in a presidential election.

In 1968, due to growing criticism of US involvement in the war in Vietnam, he announced that he would not seek re-election. Five years later he died of a heart attack.

Johnson decided to continue the work of Kennedy and carry it further. In his first speech as president he talked of a 'great society' which would declare war on poverty. To do this, he planned to improve the health of the poor and the old by providing them with a better diet and living conditions. He called for 'an immediate end to racial injustice', especially racial discrimination in employment and education. Johnson tackled areas that Kennedy had not been able to improve such as medical care for the poor.

What were Johnson's qualities?

The 'spin doctors' did not create a false image of Johnson. He was an experienced politician who knew how to get things done and how to make deals with Congress. He was far more successful than nearly any other president in getting measures passed through Congress. Also, because he was a Southerner, he knew how to deal with the Southern Democrats and overcome their opposition – especially to civil rights. Some believe his six foot five inch frame helped him to dominate others.

Johnson with one of his advisors, Abbas Fortas, 1965. Notice how Johnson towers over him.

Great Society measures

Task

1. *What was meant by the 'Great Society'?*

(If you cannot remember how to do this question refer back to the guidelines on page 76.)

Federally assisted programme
Measures helped by the central government.

Voting violations
Breaking the rules of voting.

Welfare benefits
Benefits given by the state to individuals or families, e.g. income support.

Area of reform	Key aim	Main measures	Any limitations
Civil rights	To remove all discrimination in education and employment.	*Civil Rights Act, 1964* Banned discrimination in public places, in **federally assisted programmes**, and in employment. Gave federal government new power to enforce desegregation and prosecute **voting violations**. Set up Equal Opportunity Commission. *Voting Rights Act, 1965* Appointed agents to ensure that voting procedures were carried out properly (see page 101). *Mixed marriages* In 1967, the Supreme Court declared all laws banning mixed race marriages were to be removed.	
The economy	To cut unemployment and encourage economic growth.	*Taxes* Johnson cut taxes to give consumers more money to spend and, in turn, help businesses grow and create more jobs. *Transport* He improved railways and highways. *Consumer laws* Manufacturers and shops had to label goods fairly and clearly. Consumers had the right to return faulty goods and exchange them. *Economic Opportunity Act, 1964* Tried to reduce youth unemployment by training them in new skills. Those from poor backgrounds were helped with low-interest loans so they could study at university. *Head Start Programme* Spent $1.5 billion in 1965 so that teachers could provide additional education for very young children from poor backgrounds.	
Social reform	To remove poverty in the inner cities and provide free health care for those in need.	*Medical Care Act, 1965* Free health care for those over 65 and, in the following year, Medicaid which gave free treatment to those receiving **welfare benefits**. *Food Stamp Programme* Gave families on welfare food stamps, instead of cash, to ensure they bought food. *Model Cities Act, 1966* Improved inner-city environments by clearing slums or providing parks or sports facilities. It also gave top-up payments to people on low incomes to help them pay their rent. *Elementary and Secondary Education Act, 1965* Put federal funding into improving education in poorer areas. *Minimum wage* This was increased from $1.25 an hour to $1.40. *Aid of Families and Dependent Children Act (AFDC)* Gave financial aid to 745,000 families on low incomes.	

Why was there opposition to Johnson's Great Society?

Just like Kennedy did with his policies, Johnson faced powerful opposition to his Great Society measures. This opposition, however, was distorted due to attitudes to US involvement in the war in Vietnam (1963–75).

- Republicans accused him of wasting money on welfare programmes and undermining 'rugged individualism'.
- He was accused of overspending on welfare programmes with rapid increases in health spending in particular.
- He was accused of doing too little to tackle the problems of the inner cities. In 1967, there was serious rioting in several cities including six days in Watts, the black district of Los Angeles. Thirty five people were killed and hundreds of buildings looted and burned.
- The early public enthusiasm for the Great Society faded as taxes went up to pay for his programme and inflation reached six per cent in 1968.
- In its last two years, the Great Society seemed to run out of steam and Congress cut back on its funding.
- The greatest problem for Johnson was the escalation of US involvement in the war in Vietnam (the anti-war protests are discussed further in Chapter 10). This was not only costly, meaning spending was diverted from the Great Society to paying for the war, but it led to increasing criticism of Johnson himself. His great election victory of 1964 seemed in the distant past, as many Americans celebrated his decision not to run for re-election as president in 1968.

Johnson's achievement

Johnson had done much for the poorer sections of American society. Twenty-five million Americans were given access to decent healthcare for the first time. The number of black people living below the **poverty line** fell by over fifty per cent. He greatly advanced the movement for civil rights with the Civil Rights and Voting Acts. Above all, like Roosevelt in the 1930s, he had greatly extended the role of federal government in intervening to make a difference, especially in the reduction of poverty.

Source A: President Johnson and the Great Society in the British magazine, *Punch*, in 1967. It shows him breaking up the 'Great Society'

Tasks

2. *There are no entries in the last column of the table on page 114. Make a copy of the table with the key headings and measures (no need to include the details of the measures themselves). Use the information above to write in any limitations to the measures.*

3. *Describe the key features of Johnson's 'Great Society'.*

(A seven-mark key features question. Can you remember how to answer this type of question? If not, look back to page 91.)

4. *What message is the cartoonist trying to get across in Source A?*

Examination practice

In the last section of this chapter you will learn how to answer the ten-mark essay question which appears in Section (b) of Paper 1. This is often a causation or consequence question.

Causation: asking you to explain why something happened – the reasons.

Consequence: asking you to explain the effects of an event.

Question 1 – ten-mark essay
Why was there opposition to Kennedy's 'New Frontier' and Johnson's 'Great Society'?   (10 marks)

How to answer
• First of all you need to write an introduction. This explains key terms in the question and tells the examiner the main points you intend to explain in the rest of your answer. See the example Introduction below.
• Then you need to write a series of paragraphs:
  • Begin each paragraph with an important reason.
  • Then fully explain the reason.
  • You should write three or four paragraphs.
  • Make sure you focus on the question and do not simply describe the opposition.

Now look at the example plan of the series of paragraphs on the following page and try and complete it.

Question 2 – ten-mark essay
Why did Kennedy introduce his New Frontier policy?   (10 marks)

Now have a go yourself
Always plan your answer before writing it. Make a copy of the following planning grid to help you.

> **Introduction**
>
> **First paragraph**
>
> **Link**
>
> **Second paragraph**
>
> **Link**
>
> **Third paragraph**
>
> **Link**
>
> **Fourth paragraph**
>
> **Conclusion**

Example Introduction

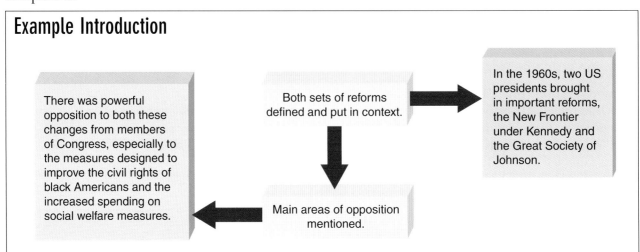

There was powerful opposition to both these changes from members of Congress, especially to the measures designed to improve the civil rights of black Americans and the increased spending on social welfare measures.

Both sets of reforms defined and put in context.

In the 1960s, two US presidents brought in important reforms, the New Frontier under Kennedy and the Great Society of Johnson.

Main areas of opposition mentioned.

Example of the series of paragraphs for Question 1

One of the main reasons for opposition was the attitude of many Southern Congressmen, even Democrats from the same party as the two presidents, who were against measures designed to improve the civil rights of black Americans.

This could be your first paragraph.

These Congressmen were often prejudiced against civil rights or feared that if they accepted any such measures of civil rights they would lose the support of many of their racist white voters. Kennedy, in particular, faced stern opposition from these politicians who prevented the passage of his Civil Rights Act. He went on a visit to Texas in an attempt to win some of them over on the day of his assassination.

The reason has been given – fully focused on the question. Now it needs to be explained in more detail.

Moreover, many Congressmen opposed both series of reforms as they saw them as a threat to the idea of 'rugged individualism'.

You will also be given credit for linking one factor (paragraph) to the next. One easy way is to practice using link words. Here are some examples: however, moreover, as a result of, this led to, therefore.

The first reason has been linked to the second. Now you would need to explain the second reason in more detail.

Have a go yourself

Overall, (A good word to use for a conclusion) there were a number of reasons for opposition to the changes brought in by the two presidents. Possibly the most serious was the fear of increased government spending to finance the social welfare measures which, in turn, meant higher taxes and the possibility of inflation. This certainly adversely affected the last year of Johnson's presidency and meant he had to curtail his reforms.

Now link this to a third reason and fully explain this reason.

Have a go yourself

All that is left is a conclusion. This should sum up your main points and give some sort of judgement. For example, for a causation question, decide which you think was the most important reason and explain why.

Who achieved most: Kennedy or Johnson?

Kennedy received the better press in the 1960s with judgements of Johnson clouded by his involvement with the war in Vietnam. What do you think?

Tasks

1. *Draw up your own balance sheet of achievements and limitations for each president. Here is a grid which may help you. You might give each president a rating using a scale of 1–5 (5 = totally successful, 1= unsuccessful) and then add up their totals. A few examples are given, although you do not have to accept these ratings.*

	Kennedy	Rating	Johnson	Rating
Economic	Cut income taxes to give people more spending money.	3		
Social				
Civil rights				
Dealing with congress			Much more skilful than Kennedy and got many measures through.	5
		Total		**Total**

2. *What is your final judgement? Who do you think was most successful? Write a paragraph of no more than 100 words explaining the reasons for your judgement.*

10 Protest movements in the 1960s and 1970s

How many times must a man look up
Before he can see the sky?
Yes, 'n' how many ears must one man have
Before he can hear people cry?
Yes, 'n' how many deaths will it take till he knows
That too many people have died?
The answer, my friend, is blowin' in the wind,
The answer is blowin' in the wind.

From the Bob Dylan song 'Blowin' in the Wind'.

Bob Dylan in 1965.

This is an extract from a protest song from Bob Dylan, one of the most popular and influential singer/songwriters of the 1960s. You will find out more about Dylan in this chapter as he had an important influence on the student protest movement. What do you think Dylan is protesting against? Pick out key words from the song that show this.

There were a range of protest movements in the USA in the 1960s and 1970s, including student, women and civil rights campaigns. They had a profound influence on the governments of the day and American society in general. In this chapter you will look at the following questions:

• Why did the student and women's movements emerge?
• How did each movement campaign?
• What influence did they have? What were their main achievements?
• What links were there between the protest movements?

Exam skills

You will be given guidance in answering the scaffolding question, in Section (b) of Paper 1 which carries 15 marks, the most of any question on either exam paper.

Why did the student movement emerge?

Source A: **A student demonstration at the University of California, Berkeley, in 1967**

Many students took a leading role in protest movements during the 1960s. This had a particularly significant impact on attitudes to the US involvement in the war in Vietnam. So why did the student movement emerge?

The legacy of the 1950s

The 1950s was a decade of frustration and anger for many young Americans. They wanted to rebel against everything, especially what their parents believed. This frustration led to the formation of teenage gangs and heavy drinking. The media seemed to fuel this rebellious attitude. Films such as *Rebel without a Cause*, featuring James Dean, led the way, followed by the emergence of rock 'n' roll, a new type of music which spread across the USA and Europe. Parents hated it, which made it even more attractive to teenagers. Elvis Presley was also very influential with his tight jeans and gyrating stage act.

The 'swinging' sixties

The attitudes of teenagers in the 1950s carried over to the next decade. It is often described as the 'swinging' sixties as the young distanced themselves even more from the older generation and its view of how the young should behave. They demanded greater freedom in everything they did: the music they listened to, the clothes they wore, the social life they led. This greater freedom, in turn, was influenced by the introduction of the contraceptive pill, which gave females much more choice over whether and when to have children and led to greater freedom in sexual behaviour, and the wider use of recreational drugs.

Source B: **Mario Savio, a Berkeley student explaining his opposition to traditional US society**

There is a time when the operation of the machine becomes so odious, makes you so sick at heart, that you can't take part; you can't even passively take part and you've got to put your bodies upon the gears and upon the wheels, upon the levers, upon all apparatus and you've got to make it stop.

Protest singers

The 1960s saw an explosion in pop music which, in turn, was an expression of this emerging youth culture, and an expression of protest against important issues of the day. On page 119 you read a verse from a Bob Dylan protest song, 'Blowin' in the Wind.' His lyrics covered the themes of the changing times, nuclear war, racism and the hypocrisy of waging war.

He was born Robert Allen Zimmerman in 1941, the grandchild of Jewish-Russian immigrants. Robert started writing poems at the age of ten and taught himself basic piano and guitar in his early teens. He was heavily influenced by contemporary rock stars such as Elvis Presley and Jerry Lee Lewis.

In 1959, he moved to Minneapolis and attended the University of Minnesota where he became even more interested in music and began performing solo at local nightspots, adopting the name of Bob Dylan. He soon dropped out of college and began writing his own songs, establishing himself with songs such as 'Blowin' in the Wind' and 'Like a Rolling Stone'. He was important for two main reasons:

• He brought poetry into mainstream rock music.
• Many of his songs attacked the injustice and intolerance of American society. He became a symbol of change.

The death of Kennedy

Kennedy's New Frontier policies (see Chapter 9) sought to harness the youth of America to his reform programme and captured the imagination and support of many. His assassination in 1963, angered and disillusioned many young Americans and drove them into protest movements.

The influence of Martin Luther King

For many young Americans, white and black, their first experience of protest was in civil rights. Martin Luther King's methods proved inspirational and many white students supported the freedom marches, freedom rides (page 96) and the sit-ins of the early and mid-1960s.

US involvement in the war in Vietnam

US involvement in the war in Vietnam divided US society, especially as the casualty list mounted and the media highlighted US atrocities against Vietnamese civilians. On the other hand, opposition to the war united the student movement. Half a million young Americans were fighting in the war and many others would be called up by the **draft** or conscription system.

The worldwide phenomena

The 1960s were also a time of student protest across the world. For example, in the later 1960s there were student protests in Northern Ireland for civil rights for Catholics and in 1968 student demonstrations in Paris were so serious they almost overthrew the government.

Tasks

1. *What can you learn from Source A about the reasons for student protest?*

2. *The reasons for student protest can be linked to each other. Do your own concept map with reasons for student protest as the central box and boxes leading off with each reason.*

• *Use different coloured pens to show links between some of the reasons.*

• *Briefly explain the link between the reasons.*

3. *Why did the student protest movement emerge?*

(This is a ten-mark essay question. Look back to pages 116–117 for further guidance on how to answer this type of question. Remember:

• *Plan your answer*

• *Make links between the reasons as you did in Task 2.)*

4. *Look again at the extract from Dylan's protest song on page 119. Now see if you can write at least one verse of your own protest song. You could set it to your own favourite type of music.*

How did the students campaign?

The SDS

One of the first protest groups to emerge in the USA was the Students for a Democratic Society (SDS). It was set up in 1959 by Tom Hayden to give students a greater say in how courses and universities were run. Hayden was a student at the University of Michigan. The SDS also wanted to help the poor and disadvantaged. It eventually formed groups in 150 colleges and universities and had 100,000 members by the end of the 1960s. Its support increased after President Johnson announced bombing raids on North Vietnam in 1965.

It first achieved national prominence when, in 1964, it organised a sit-in against a ban on political activities at the University of California at Berkeley. This was followed by a series of similar sit-ins across the USA.

> **Source A: Student protestors stage a sit-in at Columbia University, New York, April 1968**

Radical
Often a word used in politics to describe groups which hold extreme views.

Key Term

Involvement with civil rights

In 1964, student societies organised rallies and marches to support the civil rights campaign. Many were appalled at the racism in American society and were determined to expose racists in their own colleges and demanded 'free speech'.

Opposition to the war in Vietnam

This issue united the student movement. Opposition grew due to the increasing US death toll and the tactics employed by the US, including mass bombing, the use of chemical weapons and the killing of many Vietnamese civilians.

The anti-war protests reached their peak during 1968–70. In the first half of 1968, there were over a 100 demonstrations against the war, involving 400,000 students (see Source A). In 1969, 700,000 marched in Washington DC against the war. Students at these demonstrations often burned draft cards or, more seriously, the US flag which was a criminal offence. This, in turn, led to angry clashes with police.

The worst incident occurred at Kent State University, Ohio in 1970. Students were holding a peaceful protest against President Nixon's decision to bomb Cambodia as part of the Vietnam War. National Guardsmen, called to disperse the students, used tear gas to try to move them. When they refused to move shots were fired. Four people were killed and eleven injured (see Source B). The press in the USA and abroad were horrified and some 400 colleges were closed as two million students went on strike in protest against this action.

Source B: One of the students killed at Kent State University in 1970

Source C: A group of hippies wearing typical 'hippy' clothes, drumming together before the start of the Woodstock festival in 1969

Student radicalism

In the later 1960s, the student movement became more **radical** in its views. Some of its members called themselves 'Weathermen' and began to support violence to achieve their aims. They took their name from the Bob Dylan song 'You don't need a weatherman to know which way the wind blows'. They bombed army recruitment centres and government buildings. Tom Hayden disapproved of this extremism and left the movement in 1970.

The 'Hippy' movement

Other young people protested in a totally different way. They decided to 'drop out' of society and become hippies. This meant they grew their hair long, wore distinctive clothes and developed an 'alternative lifestyle'. Often they travelled round the country in buses and vans and wore flowers in their hair as a symbol of peace rather than war. Indeed their slogan was 'Make love, not war'.

They were influenced by groups such as The Grateful Dead and The Doors. The highlight of the movement came at the Woodstock and Altamont rock concerts at the end of the 1960s (see Source C). This movement was of particular concern to the older generation because:

- They refused to work.
- They experimented in drugs such as marijuana and LSD.
- Many were from middle-class and not under-privileged backgrounds. They rejected all the values that their parents believed in.

Tasks

1. *Does Source C support Sources A and B about the effects of the student movement? Explain your answer.*

(This is a cross-referencing question. Can you remember how to do it? If not, refer to page 27.)

2. *Have you ever played the game* Pictionary?

- *You have to explain the meaning of a word to someone else using an illustration.*

- *They have to guess the word you are illustrating.*

Try this out on a friend or relative with the word 'hippy' and one other new word from this section on student protest.

How was the student movement important?

What influence did the student movement have on the issues for which it campaigned, such as civil rights, greater freedom and the war in Vietnam?

Youth culture

In many respects, the most long-lasting achievement was on **youth culture** itself. By the end of the 1960s, there were profound changes in the whole lifestyle of the young. This was partly reflected in fashion, with the young becoming far more fashion-conscious and determined to move away from the 'norm' of the older generation. This is best reflected by the miniskirt, which was also a reflection of the greater **sexual permissiveness**. Teenagers became much more aware of their individuality and demanded a greater say in what they wore and did.

Vietnam

Although the SDS and student protest did not bring an end to the war in Vietnam, there is no doubt that they helped to force a shift in government policy and make the withdrawal from Vietnam much more likely. They certainly influenced President Johnson's decision not to seek re-election in 1968.

Racism

In addition, they provided greater publicity for the racism still prevalent in US society. The support of many white students for black civil rights strengthened the whole movement and showed that most American youths would no longer tolerate discrimination and segregation.

Key Terms

Sexual permissiveness
Freedom to have relationships outside marriage, often with more than one partner.

Youth culture
Beliefs, attitudes and interests of teenagers.

Middle-class origins

Finally, it should be remembered that the bulk of the students were of middle-class origin. They would have been expected to support the government in most areas. For such people to oppose the government on key issues (and in some cases oppose their families' views) was virtually unheard of and shook the older, more conservative generation.

Tasks

1. Describe the key features of the student movement.

(Remember, for this question you need at least two good-length paragraphs.)

2. Youth culture underwent great changes in the 1960s. Fashion is one example. Research one more example and prepare a one-minute talk on its key changes. Here are some possible areas of research:

- US television for the young
- the film industry
- new dance crazes
- magazines and advertisements
- changes in male youth's fashion
- other protest singers.

How did the women's movement emerge?

What was the position of women, 1945–60?

The Second World War had seen some progress in the position of women (see pages 72–73) but, for the most part, this did not continue for the generation of women who followed. Indeed, there was much media influence encouraging women to adopt their traditional family role (see Sources A and B).

Women who went out to work instead of getting married were treated with great suspicion by the rest of society. Indeed, one very influential book, *Modern Women: the Lost Sex*, actually blamed many of the social problems of the 1950s, such as teenage drinking and delinquency, on career women.

(see pages 72–73)

Key Term

Suburban
Reference to the suburbs or outskirts of a town or city.

Source B: From *The Woman's Guide to Better Living*, written in the 1950s

Whether you are a man or woman, the family is the unit to which you most genuinely belong. The family is the centre of your living. If it isn't, you've gone astray.

Source A: The typical 'mother' image

What is the role of women in society according to this source?

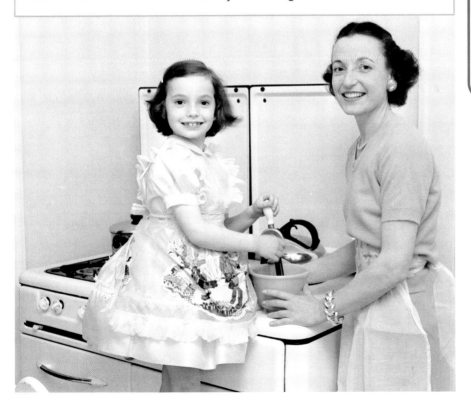

Task

1. Does Source B support the views of Source A about the position of women in the 1950s? Explain your answer.

The 1950s

In the 1950s, growing numbers of women, especially from middle-class backgrounds, began to challenge their traditional role as they became increasingly frustrated with life as a housewife. There was more to life than bringing up children and looking after their husbands. Many female teenagers were strongly influenced by the greater freedom of the 'swinging sixties' (see page 120) which, in turn, encouraged them to challenge traditional attitudes and roles. Moreover, the contraceptive pill gave females much greater choice about when or whether to have children. This could be prevented or postponed whilst a woman pursued her career.

Women were now much better educated so they could have a professional career. In 1950, there were 721,000 women at university. By 1960, this had reached 1.3 million. However, many of these had a very limited choice of career because, once they married, they were expected to devote their energies to their husband and children. Many became increasingly bored and frustrated with life as a **suburban** housewife.

The 1960s

Despite post-war attitudes, the number of women in employment continued to increase as they were a valuable source of cheap, often part-time labour for many employers. In 1950, women made up almost 29 per cent of the workforce. By 1960, this was almost 50 per cent. Eleanor Roosevelt, the widow of President Roosevelt, made an important contribution to the cause when, in 1960, she set up a commission to investigate the status of women at work.

The results were reported in 1963 and highlighted women's second class status in employment. For example, 95 per cent of company managers were men and 85 per cent of technical workers. Only seven per cent of doctors were women and even less, four per cent, lawyers. Women only earned 50 to 60 per cent of the wages of men who did the same job and generally had low-paid jobs.

Another woman, Betty Friedan, was even more influential in the emergence of the woman's movement. In 1963 she wrote *The Feminine Mystique*. Her book expressed the thoughts of many women – there was more to life than being a mother and housewife. Indeed the expression *The Feminine Mystique* was her term for the idea that a woman's happiness was all tied up with her domestic role (see Source C).

Source C: From *The Feminine Mystique*, by Betty Friedan, 1963

The problem lay buried, unspoken for many years in the minds of American women. It was a strange stirring, a sense of dissatisfaction, a yearning that women suffered in the middle of the twentieth century in the United States.

Friedan was important because she called for women to reject this 'mystique' and called for progress in female employment opportunities. She insisted that bringing up a family should be a shared role which would enable the wife to pursue her career, if she wanted. Disillusioned with the lack of progress in employment opportunities despite government legislation in 1963 and 1964 (see page 127), in 1966 she set up the National Organisation for Women (NOW).

Tasks

2. *What was meant by the 'feminine mystique'?*

(Remember how to answer this type of question? If not, look back at page 76.)

3. *Write letters to a local newspaper from two US women who have read Betty Friedan's* The Feminine Mystique *in the mid-1960s:*

• *one giving reasons in support of Friedan's views*

• *one opposing them and giving the traditional view of women.*

What did the women's movement achieve?

In the 1960s, women began to challenge their stereotyped position in society. In the table below you will see examples of the achievements and limitations of the women's movement.

Date	Key development	Achievement	Limitation
1963	Equal Pay Act	Required employers to pay women the same as men for the same job.	It did not address the issue of discrimination against women seeking jobs in the first place.
1964	Civil Rights Act	Made it illegal to discriminate on the grounds of gender.	The Equal Opportunities Commission did not take female discrimination seriously, so the Act was not fully enforced.
1966	National Organisation for Women (NOW)	This was set up by mainly white middle-class women in order to attack obvious examples of discrimination. By the early 1940s, it had 40,000 members and had organised demonstrations in American cities. They challenged discrimination in the courts and in a series of cases between 1966 and 1971, secured $30 million in back pay owed to women who had not been paid wages equal to men.	Methods too moderate and progress too slow for more extreme campaigners. Often very difficult to prove discrimination in employment through the law courts.
1972	Educational Amendment Act	This outlawed sex discrimination in education so that girls could follow exactly the same curriculum as boys. This, in turn, would give them greater career opportunities.	It took a long time for schools to change their traditional curriculum and for the benefits to filter through to the education of girls.
1972	Supreme Court	Ruled that the US Constitution did give men and women equal rights.	Many opponents of equal rights for women did not accept this.

How did the women's movement develop?

The Women's Liberation Movement

This was the name given to women who had far more radical aims than NOW. They were also known as **feminists** and were much more active in challenging discrimination. Indeed, the really extreme feminists wanted nothing to do with men. All signs of **male supremacy** were to be removed. These included male control of employment, politics and the media.

They believed that even not wearing make-up was an act of protest against male supremacy and were determined to get as much publicity for their cause as possible. For example, they burned their bras as these were also seen as a symbol of male domination. In 1968, others picketed the Miss America beauty contest in Atlantic City (see Source A) and even crowned a sheep 'Miss America'. The whole contest, they argued, degraded the position of women.

Feminist
Supporter of women's rights who believes that men and women are equal in all areas.

Male supremacy
Male control or power over females.

However, the activities of the Women's Liberation Movement did more harm than good. Their extreme actions and protests brought the wrong sort of publicity. Burning their bras in public brought ridicule to the movement and made it increasingly difficult for men and other women to take the whole issue of women's rights seriously. They were a distraction from the key issues of equal pay and better job opportunities.

The campaign to legalise abortion

Abortion was illegal in the USA. Feminists challenged this, arguing it was wrong to force women to have a child they did not want, and began to challenge this through courts of law. The most important case was Roe v Wade which lasted from 1970 to 1973. A feminist lawyer, Sarah Weddington, defended the right of one of her clients, Norma McCorvey, named Jane Roe to protect her anonymity, to have an abortion. She already had three children, who had all been taken into care, and did not want any more children. She won the right to have an abortion. The victory led to abortions becoming more readily available.

Source A: Members of the Women's Liberation Movement hold protest signs outside the Miss America Pageant (contest), in Atlantic City, 7 September 1968

1. *Why did the women's movement emerge in the USA in the 1960s?*

(A ten-mark question. Can you remember how to answer this? If not, look back at pages 116–117.)

2. *Study Source A.*

- *Devise a catchy newspaper headline for a local Atlantic City newspaper describing this scene.*

- *Write an **editorial** giving the newspaper's views of this event and the Women's Liberation Movement. Bear in mind that newspaper proprietors and editors would probably have been male.*

Opposition to the women's movement

Some women opposed the women's movement:

- Some because they believed that NOW was dominated by white middle-class females.
- Others objected to the extreme demands and methods of the Women's Liberation Movement.
- A number genuinely believed in and accepted the traditional role of women.
- Some women were anti-abortion.
- The women's movement did not seem to be doing enough to help poor women.

One of the most influential opponents was Phyllis Schafly who set up STOP ERA. Schafly was an author and had been active in politics. She had worked as a researcher for several US politicians and had stood for Congress on several occasions between 1952 and 1970. ERA stood for the Equal Rights Amendment, proposed by NOW in 1967, to change the US Constitution to guarantee women equality. Phyllis organised a highly successful campaign to stop ERA and ensured that this amendment to the constitution was delayed until 1982 when, indeed, the amendment was finally defeated by three votes. She opposed ERA because it would require women to serve in combat and thought it would have a bad influence on family life.

3. *Put together two concept maps:*

- *one showing the achievements of the women's movement*

- *the other showing its limitations.*

Here are some facts and figures to help you with this task.

In 1970, 44 per cent of men earned over $25,000 a year, while only nine per cent of women did.

The reported number of legal abortions more than doubled between 1972 and 1980.

The Feminist magazine *Ms* went on sale for the first time in 1972 and sold 250,000 copies in eight days.

Women's Studies courses appeared at universities in the early 1970s.

The US armed forces relaxed some restrictions against women in 1976, by allowing them to train at the academies at Anapolis and West Point.

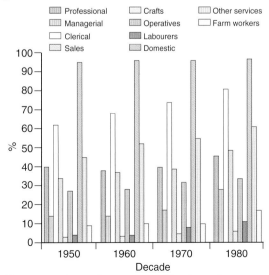

The percentage of women working in various occupations, 1950–80.

What links were there between the protest movements?

The 1960s and 1970s saw a variety of protest movements in the USA on issues as diverse as black and female civil rights, the war in Vietnam and student education. However, as you have seen so far, these protest groups generally did not act in isolation. One often led to or supported the other. For example, Martin Luther King's peaceful methods provided the inspiration for other protest groups.

Tasks

1. *Below are four pictures, each showing the main protest movements.*
- *On a piece of A3 size paper draw four boxes to represent the pictures below, and label each with the title of the movement, as below.*
- *Draw different coloured lines from one box to another to show the links between two or more of these protest movements.*
- *On your line explain the link.*
One example has been done for you.

2. *What is an acrostic? See if you can do one for the word protest:*
P
R
O
T
E
S
T

Black Civil Rights Movement

Women's Movement

A disproportionate number of black youths were drafted into the armed forces and sent to Vietnam

Student Movement

Anti-Vietnam War Movement

Examination practice

Here, and on page 141, you will be given advice on how to answer the scaffolding question. In the previous chapter you were given advice on the ten-mark question (pages 116–117). This is the other question in Section (b) of Paper 1, and is worth fifteen marks (the most of any question on Paper 1 or Paper 2). It is called the scaffolding question because the examiner not only gives you an essay-type question but also four points (or scaffolding) to help you plan and write your answer.

Question 1 – scaffolding

In what ways did the student and women's movements bring change to the USA in the 1960s and the 1970s?

You may use the following information to help you with your answer:

> The student movement
> Opposition to the war in Vietnam
> The women's movement
> The Women's Liberation Movement
>
> (15 marks)

How to answer

- Ensure you do not simply describe the four parts of the scaffolding.
- Focus on the key words in the question. Many of these questions are about change.
- Make use of each part of the scaffolding. The examiner has often put them in a logical or chronological order.
- Do a quick plan making use of each part of the scaffolding.
- Write an introduction which identifies the key areas you intend to explain in your answer. Here is a possible introduction to the above essay.

Example
In the 1960s and 1970s the student and women's movements brought important changes to American society, with genuine progress in women's pay and employment and the emergence of a distinctive youth culture.

- After your introduction, write at least one good-length paragraph on each part of the scaffolding.

- Begin each paragraph with a sentence which focuses on the question. Here is an example.

Example
The women's movement brought about significant improvements in the economic and social position of women in US society.

You would now have to give a developed explanation of this factor focusing on how it brought change to the USA.

- Try to make links between each of the scaffolding factors. Remember the link words that you used in the ten-mark question (see page 116). Below is a possible link between the student movement and protests against the war in Vietnam.

Example
The student movement not only campaigned for greater freedom in society and on their campuses, but also played a prominent part in the opposition to the war in Vietnam.

- Look back to the linking exercise you did on page 130 to help you to make links between the factors.
- If you can think of one additional factor not mentioned by the examiner, write a paragraph on this. Make sure the examiner is aware that this is an additional factor. One possibility for this essay could be the hippy movement.

Example
The hippy movement also brought important changes as it emphasised the importance of peace and love and seriously questioned the idea of war, such as US involvement in Vietnam, as a solution to the problems of the time.

You would have to give a more developed explanation of the role of the hippies, focusing on the changes they brought.

Now look at the advice for a conclusion on the next page.

• Write a conclusion making your final judgement on the key issue, for example the extent of and/or reasons for change. An example is given below.

Example

The protest movements brought important changes to American society. Above all else, they challenged traditional and conservative views of the position of young, female and/or black Americans and influenced successive governments into far reaching reforms.

Now have a go yourself

Answer question 1 on page 131. Make a copy of the following grid and use it to help you plan your answer.

Introduction

First paragraph – first scaffolding factor
Introduce the first scaffolding factor and then fully explain it. Make a judgement about how much change it bought. Do the same for each factor you explain.

Link with second factor

Second paragraph – second scaffolding factor

Link with third factor

Third paragraph – Third scaffolding factor

Link with fourth factor

Fourth paragraph – Fourth scaffolding factor

Link with extra factor

Fifth paragraph – extra factor

Conclusion

The Watergate scandal and its impact

11

Source A A cartoon in the *Washington Post*, 1973. What message is the cartoonist trying to get across?

Once upon a time there were some naughty men. Let's call them CREEP. They broke into someone's office. They were caught and put on trial. Soon the person at the top of the country was accused of being involved. He said he was innocent. Then it was found that there were tape recordings which could prove he was involved. The top person refused to hand these over. Eventually he was forced to and was shown to have lied. He faced a serious trial. To avoid this he had to give up his job. Nobody lived happy ever after.

Is this fact or fiction?

In this chapter we will look at the amazing event of the 1970s which rocked American society – the Watergate scandal. You will need to answer the following important questions:

- What caused the scandal?
- Why was President Nixon involved?
- What were the key events of the scandal?
- Why did Nixon resign?
- What effects did the scandal have on the USA?
- Did Nixon have any other more positive achievements?

Exam skills
You will be given the opportunity to practice questions on all the different types of questions you will have to answer on Paper 1.

What caused the Watergate scandal?

Biography Richard Nixon, 1913–94

Nixon was born in California in 1913 and became a brilliant scholar and lawyer. He was elected to Congress and, in 1950, won a seat in the Senate. Nixon began to make a name for himself in the McCarthy anti-communist witch hunts (see pages 82–83). In 1952 he was Eisenhower's running mate for the presidency and became his vice-president, 1953–61. He was narrowly defeated by Kennedy in the 1960 presidential election campaign but was successful in 1968 and again in 1972. He died in 1994.

Key Terms

FBI

Stands for Federal Bureau of Investigation. Set up to investigate organised crime.

CIA

Stands for Central Investigation Agency. The secret service responsible for security inside and outside the USA. Organises spying.

Nixon giving his well-known victory salute during his presidential campaign in 1968.

CREEP

In 1968, Richard Nixon, the Republican candidate, was elected president. In 1972 he would have to seek re-election. Concerned that he might not be re-elected, he set up CREEP, 'Committee to Re-elect the President'. It was led by John Mitchell, a close adviser to Nixon, who was encouraged to use any tactics he saw fit to ensure Nixon's re-election, including dirty tricks or illegal methods. Sixty million dollars were illegally collected to fight this campaign, with $350,000 set aside for these dirty tricks, including the idea of 'bugging' the Democrat offices at Watergate.

The break-in

On 17 June, five members of CREEP were arrested for breaking into the Watergate offices. It soon became obvious that they were not ordinary burglars but were trying to plant electronic bugging devices. At this stage no one made any direct connection to CREEP or Nixon.

The *Washington Post* reporters

Two reporters from the *Washington Post,* Carl Bernstein and Bob Woodward, carried out their own investigations and uncovered some facts which proved very embarrassing to the White House. First of all one of the burglars was an ex-member of the **CIA**. More seriously, all five burglars were employed by CREEP and the CREEP fund was controlled at the White House. The reporters also publicised other illegal activities financed by CREEP.

The FBI

The **FBI** now became involved and carried out an investigation of CREEP's activities. It found that CREEP had organised a massive campaign of spying on Nixon's opponents and used every tactic possibly to disrupt their campaign, including trying to find out any scandals involving the leading Democrat politicians.

George McGovern, the Democrat candidate for the presidency in 1972, also accused Nixon of involvement in the break-in. In a speech during the presidential campaign of 1972 he said:

*'The Republicans tried to place listening devices in our campaign office. They even plotted a disruption of their own Republican **convention** so they could blame it on the Democrats. The men who have ordered this political sabotage, who have invaded our offices in the middle of the night – all these men work for Mr Nixon. Most of them he hired himself. They act on his behalf, and they all accept his orders. And he has blocked any independent investigations.'*

Nixon strongly denied all involvement by himself and his advisers. There were even claims that White House staff had been bribed to keep quiet, with one person receiving $25,000. At this stage, few took much notice of the story and Nixon won a landslide victory in the 1972 presidential election.

The trial of the burglars

In January 1973, the Watergate burglars went on trial and all were convicted. In March, when they were sentenced, one of the burglars, James McCord, claimed in court that there had been a White House cover-up and even that witnesses had lied during the trial.

Again, Nixon denied all knowledge of the break-in or any cover-up and even went on television to announce that 'there can be no whitewash at the White House'. He did admit, however, in April 1973, that his top two advisers, Bob Haldeman and John Ehrlichman, had been involved in the break-in but had now resigned. He also announced an investigation with Archibald Cox appointed as special Watergate prosecutor.

Tasks

1. *What can you learn from Source A (on page 133) about the Watergate scandal?*

2. *Why do you think that few people at the time believed McGovern's accusations?*

3. *You are one of the two reporters from the* Washington Post *who discover the links between the burglars and CREEP. Put together a headline and leading article that you suggest your editor should use.*

The plot thickens

Throughout the summer of 1973, there were more twists and turns to the scandal. The Senate held its own investigation, headed by Senator Sam Ervin. The Senate Watergate Committee heard televised evidence between May and November 1973 and it became increasingly obvious that senior White House officials had been involved. One of them, John Dean, claimed there had been a cover-up and Nixon had directed it. Nixon still denied all involvement.

The battle over the White House tapes

The most significant evidence was from one White House aide who told the Senate Committee that in 1971 Nixon had installed a tape-recording system in the White House and that all the President's conversations had been taped.

Both the Senate Committee and Cox asked Nixon to hand over the tapes. He refused, insisting it would breach national security and sacked Cox on 20 October 1973. The Attorney General resigned in protest. The new prosecutor, Leon Jaworksi, also demanded the tapes. Nixon handed over seven of the nine tapes but they had been heavily edited – one of them had eighteen minutes missing. Jaworski then appealed to the Supreme Court which ordered Nixon to hand over all the tapes.

Source A: **A 1974 cartoon about Nixon and the tapes**

Finally, Nixon handed over the tapes which revealed that he had been involved in the dirty tricks campaign and had repeatedly lied throughout the investigation. The tapes also shocked the nation because of the language used by Nixon. He frequently used foul language and made ethnic insults. Any foul language was indicated by 'expletive deleted' which occurred at frequent intervals.

Source B: **From the tapes of 21 March 1973, describing attempts at a cover-up**

Dean: That's right. Plus there is a real problem in raising money. Mitchell has been working on raising money. He is one of the ones with the most to lose. But there is no denying the fact that the White House, in Ehrlichman and Haldeman, are involved in the early money decisions.
President: How much money do you need?
Dean: I would say these people are going to cost a million dollars over the next two years.
President: You could get a million dollars. You could get it in cash. I know where it could be gotten. But the question is who the hell would handle it. Any ideas?

The end of the scandal

In July 1974, Congress decided to impeach Nixon. This meant he would be put on trial with the Senate acting as the jury. He was accused of:

- Obstructing justice by trying to cover up the role of the White House in the Watergate Burglary.
- Using the FBI and the CIA to harass any critics of the government. He even tried to stop the setting up of an FBI investigation into the Watergate scandal.
- Defying Congress by his refusal to hand over the tapes.

An opinion poll revealed that 66 per cent of the US public agreed with his impeachment. Nixon would almost certainly have been found guilty, on the evidence of the tapes. On 8 August 1974, Nixon resigned to avoid being impeached. He was the first president to resign and Gerald Ford was sworn in as his successor. Ford issued a decree pardoning Nixon for any criminal acts that he had taken part in.

A television broadcast of President Nixon's resignation.

Tasks

4. *Study Source A (page 136). What message is the cartoonist trying to get across?*

5. *Study Source B (page 136). Why would the evidence in this extract incriminate Nixon?*

6. *Draw a timeline showing the key events of the scandal. Begin with the break-in on 17 June 1972 and finish with Nixon's resignation, 8 August 1974.*

7. *You have just watched Nixon's resignation speech (see the photo above). Put together a mobile phone text message informing a friend of what you have seen. You may use 'text language'. Remember your word limit – with most mobile phones it is 144 letters.*

What effects did the scandal have?

Key changes after Watergate

After Watergate, Congress brought in a series of measures to reduce the powers of the President.

Campaign contributions
Money given to political parties to pay for election campaigns.

Key Term

The Election Campaign Act, 1974

This set limits on **campaign contributions** to prevent corruption.

The War Powers Act, 1973

This required the president to consult with Congress before sending American troops into prolonged action.

The Privacy Act, 1974

This allowed citizens to have access to any files that the government may have had on them.

The Congressional Budget and Impoundment Control Act, 1974

This meant that the president could not use government money for his own purposes.

Did the scandal seriously weaken the USA?

Yes

- The scandal had serious repercussions for American society. Even now scandals are generally given the nickname 'gate' after the name of the scandal, for example 'Irangate' scandal.
- It utterly destroyed Nixon's reputation. He was seen an untrustworthy and was given the nickname 'Tricky Dicky'. For many years after, the Watergate scandal overshadowed all his other achievements.
- Some 31 Nixon advisers went to prison for Watergate-related offences.
- It greatly undermined people's confidence in politics and politicians. Were all politicians as corrupt as Nixon or was he a one-off? In 1976 Americans voted for the presidential candidate they could trust, the Democrat Jimmy Carter. He promised never to tell a lie.
- The scandal damaged the reputation of the USA abroad and made the USA a laughing stock. The USSR was able to use it as an example of the corruption of the capitalist system. It also came at the same time that US forces were being pulled out of the conflict in Vietnam, an action that further undermined American self-confidence.

No

Others, however, argued that the Watergate scandal actually strengthened the USA.

- Watergate seemed to show how well the legal and political system worked. Nixon had been found out and forced to resign.
- The balances of the US Constitution also worked well. Ultimately, the Supreme Court had carried out its ultimate function and kept a check on the position of the president
- It led to a series of measures which rightly limited the powers of the presidency and 'cleaned up' politics.
- Lack of confidence in politics and the presidency was short-lived as was shown by the early popularity of President Carter at the end of the 1970s.

Tasks

1. *What were the main consequences of the Watergate scandal?*

2. *Do you think the Watergate scandal strengthened or weakened the US political system? Give your views with reasons in less than 100 words.*

What were Nixon's other achievements?

Nixon's presidency is overshadowed by the Watergate scandal but there were other achievements, especially abroad.

Social and economic policies

There was some progress, especially in civil rights, with more than 400,000 black Americans at college by 1970 and more entering politics. By 1971, there were thirteen black congressmen and 81 black mayors. Yet this was largely achieved despite Nixon, who showed little interest in domestic politics.

His economic policies were not successful. He inherited a rise in prices and tried to reduce this by strict control of borrowing by the US people and business. This, however, did not help the growth of the US economy as it restricted business. Prices continued to rise, as Nixon failed to control wage rises, as did unemployment. He did reduce taxes but this, also, increased inflation.

He rejected proposals to set up childcare centres for mothers who needed to work but he did increase welfare benefits.

Achievements abroad

Nixon had more lasting achievements in his foreign policy. In his election campaign of 1968 he had promised to get the USA out of the conflict in Vietnam. He kept to his promise, introducing a policy of **Vietnamisation** by which US forces were withdrawn and the defence of South Vietnam was left in the hands of its own armed forces. He also ended the very unpopular draft system.

Perhaps his greatest achievement was in relations with China. He worked hard to improve relations with China, especially as China was undergoing a period of strained relations with the Soviet Union. Improved **Sino**–American relations drove a further wedge between China and the USSR. This was nicknamed 'ping-pong' diplomacy and included new trade and sporting links, with Nixon even visiting China.

Key Terms

Sino
Another word for Chinese.

Vietnamisation
Nixon's policy of withdrawing US troops from South Vietnam and leaving South Vietnamese, with US support, to repel the threat from the Vietcong.

Nixon's visit to China in 1972. Here he is meeting the Chinese leader, Mao Zedong.

Task

If you consult any book of brief biographies of the twentieth century you will find the name of Richard Nixon. The entry will be dominated by the Watergate scandal. Put together your own one-paragraph entry trying to give a more balanced view of Nixon's career and achievements.

Examination practice

In the last section of this chapter you are given the opportunity to practise the skills you have in answering questions in the style of Sections (a) and (b) of Paper 1.

Section (a)

1. What was meant by 'CREEP'? (3 marks)
2. Describe the key events of the Watergate scandal. (7 marks)
   (You could use the timeline you completed in the task on page 137 to help you with this question.)
3. What consequences did the Watergate scandal have for the US political system? (5 marks)

Section (b)

Remember you will have to write two essays:

• A ten-mark essay question often on cause or consequence.
• A scaffolding question which could be on key events or changes.

Ten-mark essay question

Why was there a scandal in the years 1972–74 which eventually forced the resignation of Nixon as president? (10 marks)

First you need to plan your answer. Here is a planning grid. Make a copy and use it to write down the key points you will develop.

> Introduction
>
> First paragraph – first reason
>
> Link to second paragraph
>
> Second paragraph – second reason
>
> Link to third paragraph
>
> Third paragraph – third reason
>
> Link to fourth paragraph
>
> Fourth paragraph – fourth reason
>
> Conclusion

Scaffolding question

What changes took place in the USA during Nixon's presidency, 1968 to 1974?
   You may use the following:

> The Watergate scandal
> Economic and social change
> The war in Vietnam
> 'Ping-pong' diplomacy (15 marks)

Make a copy of the following plan and write in the key points you will explain.

Introduce the first scaffolding factor and then fully explain it. Make a judgement about how much change it bought. Do the same for each factor you explain.

> Introduction
>
> First paragraph – Watergate
>
> Link to second paragraph
>
> Second paragraph – Economic and social change
>
> Link to third paragraph
>
> Third paragraph – The war in Vietnam
>
> Link to fourth paragraph
>
> Fourth paragraph – 'Ping-pong' diplomacy
>
> Link to fifth paragraph
>
> Fifth paragraph – Anything else about the period?
>
> Conclusion

Remember to answer the question – you are not being asked to describe Nixon's policies. The question is about the changes that Nixon's policies brought in US society in the period of his presidency. How different was the USA after Nixon's presidency to the period before?

Glossary

Alphabet Agencies Those bodies set up in the New Deal to tackle the problems of the Depression. They were abbreviated and known by the letters of the alphabet, for example the Civilian Conservation Corps was the CCC.

Armistice An agreement for a temporary end to hostilities.

Attorney General Chief legal officer of the US government.

Back to normalcy Harding's slogan promised a return to the more carefree days of 1917 – before the US entered the First World War.

Balance the budget Ensuring that the government does not spend more than it raises in taxes.

Basic human rights Such as free speech, assumed to belong to all people everywhere.

Battle of the Bulge Hitler's last assault on allied forces in the West.

Bolsheviks The political group led by Lenin. They believed in communism.

Bond A certificate of debt issued in order to raise funds. It carries a fixed rate of interest.

Boom Time when the economy is doing well, with a growth in production, exports, employment and often wages.

Bull market A time when share prices are rising.

Campaign contributions Money given to political parties to pay for election campaigns.

Capitalist country A country in which businesses are owned privately and people are able to make a profit.

CIA Central Investigation Agency, the secret service responsible for security inside and outside the USA. Organises spying.

Civil rights The campaign for equal social, economic and political rights and opportunities.

Collective bargaining Negotiation of workers, represented by union leaders, with employers.

Communism Political theory which put forward the idea of state ownership of industry and agriculture.

Communist A believer in the theory that society should be classless, private property abolished, and land and businesses owned collectively. Following the Communist Revolution in Russia in 1917, there had been a growing fear that communism might spread to the USA and destroy the system of government.

Congress The USA equivalent of parliament is Congress. Congress is split into two parts, the Senate and the House of Representatives. Anyone elected to either house is called a congressman.

Congress of Racial Equality (CORE) Established in 1942 by James Farmer. CORE was the first organisation in the USA to use the tactic of sit-ins.

Conscripted Where males of a certain age (usually 18–41) have to serve in the armed forces for a period of time.

Conservative Democrats Democrats who did not want much change.

Conservatives Those who wished to maintain existing approaches to running the economy.

Constitution The rules under which a country is governed.

Consumer goods Manufactured items purchased by people.

Convention A large meeting.

Credit The facility of borrowing money over a given period.

Creditor One to whom a financial debt is owed.

Democrat Someone belonging to the Democratic Party, one of the two parties in the USA, which tended to follow policies of government intervention and favoured measures to improve health, welfare and education.

Democratic Party One of the two main political parties.

Depression A period of extended and severe decline in a nation's economy, marked by low production and high unemployment.

Desegregation Removal of the policy of separation.

Discrimination Unfair treatment of individuals because of their gender, race or religious beliefs.

Disenfranchisement Taking away the right to vote from an individual.

Dixiecrats Democrat Party senators from the southern states.

Draft US method of recruitment into the armed forces. It was compulsory for men (youths) who reached the age of eighteen to serve in the armed forces.

Editorial Often the main article written by the editor of the newspaper.

Enfranchise To give an individual the right to vote.

FBI Federal Bureau of Investigation set up to investigate organised crime.

Federal government The central government of the USA, which is based in Washington DC.

Federally assisted programme Measures helped by the central government.

Feminist Supporter of women's rights who believes that men and women are equal in all areas.

Fifth Amendment Part of the US constitution which allows the accused person in a trial not to be forced to give testimony.

Fireside chat When Roosevelt spoke to the nation it was assumed that people sat by the fire as they listened to him. The image was of a cosy friendly chat.

General Motors One of the largest car manufacturers in the USA.

Governor The elected head of a state within the USA.

Hobo Wandering unemployed workman seeking a job.

House of Representatives The lower chamber of the US Congress.

Import duties Taxes placed on goods brought from foreign countries.

Income tax Payment from wages/salaries to the government treasury.

Industrialist Someone who owns and/or runs an industry or factory.

Infrastructure The key services upon which the economy depends, such as roads, railways, water supplies, electricity.

Integrated combat units Combat units including all soldiers irrespective of race.

Internment camps Effectively prison camps.

Interstate commerce Trade between two or more states.

Laissez-faire A policy of no direct government interference in the economy.

Liberals Those who were prepared to introduce reforms in order to overcome economic problems.

Male supremacy Male control or power over females.

Mass production The manufacture of the same item on an assembly line, where the workers carry out the same task as the item passes before them.

Migrate To move from one part of the country to another.

Militant Aggressive in the support of a cause.

Minimum wage The lowest wage per hour that someone can be paid.

Munitions Ammunition/weapons produced for the armed forces.

Nationalise When the government takes on the running of an organisation.

Negro The word used at that time for black Americans.

Poverty line The income level at which a family is unable to meet its basic needs.

Price-fixing Agreement to charge the same or similar price for goods.

Provenance This means the information given above or below the source, such as who wrote it and when.

Quaker Name given to the religious group devoted to principles of peace, plainness of speech and dress.

Race riots Riots by one race against another.

Radical Often a word used in politics to describe groups which hold extreme views.

Rationing Introduced by the government to avoid shortages in key commodities. Families/individuals were restricted in what they could buy.

Recession A period of declining productivity and reduced economic activity.

Relief agency Body set up to help those suffering as a result of the Depression.

Republican Supporter of the Republican Party. Its main ideas were to keep taxes low, limit the powers of the federal government, follow policies which favoured business and encourage people to be self-sufficient.

Rugged individualism The American ideal that individuals are responsible for their own lives without help from anyone else; they stand or fall by their own efforts.

Secretary for labour Responsible for policies dealing with employer/worker relations and working conditions.

Segregation Separating groups due to their race or religion. This could include separate housing, education, health treatment, access to public buildings.

Segregationists Those who believed in the policy of separation of races.

Senate The Upper House of the US Congress (parliament).

Senator Member of the senate. There are two senators per state in the USA.

Separatism Keeping races apart.

Sexual permissiveness Freedom to have relationships outside marriage, often with more than one partner.

Sino Another word for Chinese.

Sit-in A form of civil disobedience in which demonstrators occupy a public place and, as a protest, refuse to move.

SNCC Student Non-violent Co-ordinating Committee – founded by students at Shaw University, North Carolina. Its aim was to attack examples of discrimination and by peaceful methods demand equality for black Americans.

Socialist Those who want much greater government involvement in the economy and society.

Socialist state A state in which the government, not private individuals, controls the means of production.

Spin doctors A relatively recent term referring to the media people employed to provide a positive image of a government or individual.

State legislature The law-making body within the individual state.

Stock market The place where stocks and shares were bought and sold on a daily basis.

Stocks and shares Certificates of ownership in a company.

Suburban Reference to the outskirts of a town or city.

Superpowers At the end of the war, the USA and USSR were so powerful in military and economic terms that they had left all other countries behind.

Supreme Court The highest federal court in the USA consisting of nine judges chosen by the president, who make sure that the president and Congress obey the rules of the Constitution.

The New Deal The name given to the policies introduced by President Roosevelt in the 1930s to solve the problems created by the Depression.

Thrifty Careful with spending.

Unconstitutionally Breaking the rules or constitution.

Urban ghettos Town/city area consisting of a minority who live there because of social and economic pressures.

USSR/Soviet Union Name given to Russia after the Bolshevik Revolution.

Veto The right of the president to block a piece of legislation.

Vietnamisation Nixon's policy of withdrawing US troops from South Vietnam and leaving the South Vietnamese, with US support, to repel the threat from the Vietcong.

Voting violations Breaking the rules of voting.

Wall Street Stock Exchange New York's stock market was based here.

Welfare benefits Benefits given by the state to individuals or families, e.g. income support.

Youth culture Beliefs, attitudes and interests of teenagers.

Index